Undeniable Wisdom

A Pathway of a Biblical Intelligence and Insight

W. A. Tyrrell

Undeniable Wisdom

A Pathway of a Biblical Intelligence and Insight

Copyright 2022 by Wynette A. Tyrrell

ISBN 978-1-947741-73-7

Published by Kingdom Publishing, LLC
1350 Blair Drive, Odenton, MD 21113

Printed in the USA

All rights reserved. No part of this book may be reproduced, stored in retrieval system, or transmitted in any form or by any means—electronic, mechanical, photocopy, recording, or otherwise—except for brief quotations in printed reviews, without the prior written permission of the author.

Unless otherwise indicated, all Scripture quotations are taken from the King James Version (public domain). Scripture quotations marked "NASB" are taken from the New American Standard Bible®, Copyright © 1960, 1962, 1963, 1968, 1971, 1972, 1973, 1975, 1977, 1995 by The Lockman Foundation. Used by permission. www.Lockman.org. Scripture quotations marked "NCV" are taken from the New Century Version. Copyright © 2005 by Thomas Nelson, Inc. Used by permission. All rights reserved. Bible text from the New Century Version® is not to be reproduced in copies or otherwise by any means except as permitted in writing by Thomas Nelson Publishers, Attn: Bible Rights and Permissions, P.O. Box 141000, Nashville, TN 37214-1000. http://www.nelsonbibles.com/ Scripture quotations marked (NIV) are taken from the Holy Bible, New International Version®, NIV®. Copyright © 1973, 1978, 1984 by Biblica, Inc.™ Used by permission of Zondervan. All rights reserved worldwide. http://www.zondervan.com. Scripture quotations marked "NKJV" are taken from the New King James Version. Copyright © 1982 by Thomas Nelson, Inc. Used by permission. All rights reserved. Bible text from the New King James Version® is not to be reproduced in copies or otherwise by any means except as permitted in writing by Thomas Nelson, Inc., Attn: Bible Rights and Permissions, P.O. Box 141000, Nashville, TN 37214-1000. http://www.nelsonbibles.com/ Scripture quotations marked (NLT) are taken from the Holy Bible, New Living Translation, copyright © 1996, 2004, 2007 by Tyndale House Foundation. Used by permission of Tyndale House Publishers, Inc., Carol Stream, Illinois 60188. All rights reserved. http://www.newlivingtranslation.com/ http://www.tyndale.com Scripture quotations marked "ESV" are from the ESV Bible® (The Holy Bible, English Standard Version®), copyright © 2001 by Crossway Bibles, a publishing ministry of Good News Publishers. Used by permission. All rights reserved. http://www.crossway.org

DEDICATION

"To the Only Wise God, our Savior, be glory and majesty, dominion, and power. And to Him who is able to keep you from falling, and to present you faultless, before the presence of His glory with exceeding joy, both now and forever."

Amen

(Jude 24:25)

Acknowledgment

To: "My sons"

I pray that the Love of the Father God and the blessings of His son, Jesus Christ our Savior and the Holy Spirit be ever present with you.

My love and my faith in the Lord Jesus Christ have brought great peace in my heart. I thank the Lord for bestowing these awesome gifts that shine as beacons of God's amazing love.

I thank you Lord for your promises are sure, and there is no failure with God.

(2 Corinthians 1:20)

TABLE OF CONTENT

Dedication

Acknowledgement

Introduction – The Principal Thing! 1

Chapter 1 – A Curiosity for Wisdom 9

Chapter 2 – Undeniable Wisdom! 17

Chapter 3 – The Wisdom of Jesus Christ 27

Chapter 4 – The Wisdom Phenomenon 43

Chapter 5 – The Foundation of Wisdom 51

Chapter 6 – Wisdom Likened to a Woman! 59

Chapter 7 – The Astuteness of Divine Wisdom 69

Chapter 8 – The Favor of God 77

Chapter 9 – Wisdom is Transferable 87

Chapter 10 – The Curiosity of Job 99

Chapter 11 – The Treasures of Wisdom 105

Chapter 12 – The Ungodly Wisdom 119

Chapter 13 – The Distinction of the Imprudent 131

Chapter 14 – The Peculiarity of the Wise 141

Chapter 15 – The Access to Wisdom 149

Chapter 16 – Wisdom is a Medicine 159

Chapter 17 – A Divine Intelligence 165

Chapter 18 – Walking in Divine Wisdom 173

About the Author 179

Introduction

The Principal Thing!

The highpoint of this book is written of an undeniable wisdom. There are theological perspectives that activated this motivation to pursue an extensive understanding of wisdom. The subject of the origins of wisdom has accentuated in the verse that says, "Wisdom is the principal thing." There may be many questions regarding the aspect of attaining much wisdom. There are biblical scriptures written which gave an outlook of what God had to say about wisdom. Each topic has enlightened the awareness based upon the fundamentals that relates to the natural and spiritual wisdom that comes from God.

The deliberation of many questions to a certain degree is found in the book of Proverbs. These verses of scripture had gratified much of my curiosity through its form of integral design of true wisdom. The text establishes that wisdom can be referenced to the human or the animal kingdom and their habitation. The human performance could reflect an involvement with wisdom, as the insight towards a reverence to God as the Creator produces progression of moral principles.

The representation of God Himself is Wisdom. As theologians have excluded any theory that states otherwise; for they have demarcated wisdom as having a charisma. The fact that God is All-knowing validates His persona of an infinite wisdom. The word of God is the written portion of the illustration of His wisdom which can never be nullified. I have considered that there is absolutely nothing unaware to God, the creator of the universe. He has no need to study books or explore theories like mankind does.

The fact that God loves writing is featured in His reliable plethora of books. In His divine wisdom, the bible classifies that God is an Author. In Jewish history there are manuscripts of the journeys of Moses and the children of Israel; and a detailed account of all their experiences throughout the forty years. He rehearsed

God's instructions from Egypt to the Promise land, we could read this in the book of (Deuteronomy, chapter 28). Through Moses' writings, he made a great representation of how God's love for details is significant to Him. God wanted their events of the past and the present to be depicted as a cultural history for the families of Israel from generation to generation. The tribal history of Israel is very important information for His people to walk with the Lord God. One of the Jewish customs is the priestly blessings of the Levite tribe, which is significant to God, in such a way that it reveals His love for Israel (Numbers 6:23-27). God had instructed Moses that one of the priestly duties was to speak a blessing over the people: *"And God said, they (the Priest) will place my name on the children of Israel and the Priest will bless the people, and I will bless them."* There is a customary prayer that the Jewish Rabbis pray over the people that says, "The Lord bless you and keep you!" It is known as the prayer of the Priestly Blessing, or the Aaronic Blessing. The Sages say that this was done for thousands of generations; and it is their practice even today. Therefore, because Moses did write all the commands of God, we as believers have this prayer to recite.

The scriptures revealed that God in His divine wisdom had inspired the prophets to record everything that He gave as instructions. All the prophets including Jeremiah and Isaiah were instructed by the divine inspiration of God to write the prophetic words they received. According to the historians, there is written proof that Jesus Christ, our Messiah was born of a Jewish descendant; His birth was out of the tribe of Judah, and His lineage was of a priestly and kingly anointing. Even today, there are clear depictions which identify its source with the nature of God, in the writing of manuscripts, records of cultural and family history, and chronological accounts of events.

John the Revelator revealed that God had instructed him to write about the importance of the two books that he saw in Heaven (Revelation 5:1). He alluded that there is a written record-keeping system in heaven and in those books were information of records of people in this earth. According to John, there are two books

INTRODUCTION

which were identified as the book of Life for the righteous, and the book of Judgment or Death for those who chose the path of impure living. He indicated that in the vision he saw other books, and there were books of those that were dead, great, and small, standing before the throne, and the books were opened. This was intriguing; it gave a distinct overview to what records are kept for every person in God's possession (Revelation 20:11-15).

Moreover, the prophet Malachi forewarned the children of Israel that he saw in a vision that there was a book of Remembrance written, and these books were kept in the presence of God (Malachi 3:16). In one of the many visions that Daniel received, he conferred that one of the books God has in His possession was the book of Truth (Daniel 10:21). King David's life experiences produced writings of his many encounters with the mercy of God. As he acknowledged that God was his protector, he also proclaimed that all his days were ordained by God, and they were written in His book (Psalm 139:16). The Psalmist David recognized that all circumstances he had faced were designed for his purpose in life.

The attitude of the human mind desires is to understand the truth, and to achieve a successful life. In fact, the obligation to desire wisdom and understanding which comes from God is an undeniable inadequacy. Our primary thought is foremost great wealth, and accomplishment. According to (Joshua 1:8) the people who chose wisdom is declared to have great prosperity and health. The Bible says that King Solomon chose wisdom over wealth, and the Lord added the gift of great wealth. Moreover, in all biblical circles King Solomon's name is greatly mentioned as an example in this respect.

The apostle Paul recognized that in himself, the philosophies of God were beyond his comprehension, and he declared, *"Eyes have not seen, nor ears heard, nor have entered into the heart of man all the things that God has prepared for those who love Him"* (1 Corinthians 2:9). There is another translation that says, "No eyes have seen, no ears have heard, neither fathom, nor understand the beauty and awesomeness of heaven. According to the word of God, the basis of the wholesome life is entwined in the gift of wisdom. These phrases give clarity that the human mind cannot perceive the goodness and mercy of God towards His creation.

A few years ago, I read a scientific documentary which stated that there are talented cases of intelligence, which they have deemed mysterious. They acknowledged that there is a source from the God above. They have also documented that some humans, and most intelligent animals, do have an exceptional capability to display an irrefutably origin of wisdom. Notably, it is stated that all male and female species do consist of diverse capabilities; and hence, their honorable wisdom was equated to a spiritual existence. In some cases, an individual who experience challenges in life are usually unpredictable in their wisdom. Many scientists refer to the unexplainable with speculation, as they label such divine intelligence to the peculiarity of the circumstance. In other circumstances, those persons that have much wisdom and discernment felt indebted, and they concurred that their gift was from God.

There is an illustration of some animals that accomplished task which could not be done without wisdom from God as mentioned in one of the chapters. What seemed challenging to the natural man is that some of those animals physically attained as their adaptability and preparation for expediting a particular task appears captivating. The testimony of their amazing displays could be declared as wisdom from above. There are interesting principles of wisdom in relation to mankind, and their choice of a moral quality also discussed in this book. There are distinctive principles specified by God to the natural and spiritual wisdom. The prerequisite of the foundation of wisdom is God. The word of God admonishes us to get wisdom, and along with all your accomplishment, get insight.

> *"Wisdom is the principal thing; therefore, get wisdom: and with all your getting get understanding"*
> (Proverbs 4:7)

INTRODUCTION

The bible declares that "the fear of God is the beginning of wisdom, and the knowledge of the Holy One is understanding" (Proverbs 9:10). The interpretation of this phrase can be clarified as, "Wisdom is the principal thing." The Sages say that the principle of wisdom could be referred to as an attitude of morals toward an ethical behavior of life. The phenomenon of wisdom encompasses the personal relationship of the human and the Lord Jesus Christ. Moreover, wisdom enhances our everyday life in many ways as it gives the natural man an advantage of knowledge. It is encouraged and instructed that all mankind should desire the divine wisdom to encompass their natural ways of life.

The two categories of wisdom conferred in the book are a Godly and an Ungodly wisdom. The simple explanation is that a Godly wisdom is the knowledge that is accomplished by following the guidelines of the Headship of God, and by understanding His word. The purpose of wisdom can introduce someone to the beginning of knowledge for the things of God (Proverbs 1:7). The Hebraic word for wisdom is *"Chokmah"* and it is derived from the verb *"chakam"* which means *"to be wise, to be filled with knowledge, or to be skillful."* This wisdom is biblical, and it is referred to as the divine gift (Exodus 35:35). The fact that wisdom does exist is the fundamental aspect of knowledge, and it is enlightening to say that true wisdom cannot function without the Spirit of God.

The characteristics of ungodly wisdom are one of the topics in the book. The scriptures tell us that this wisdom was categorized as an act of perverting godly wisdom. All ungodly wisdom is correlated to the acts of disobedience and the sinfulness of mankind, which leads to wickedness and craftiness. These ungodly character traits can be verbally or physically revealed. The Apostle Paul warned the believers not to be unaware of the principles of wisdom. He emphasized that there are two categories of wisdom and he gave illustrations on how the believer needs to act within the body of Christ. His advice is beneficial to our spiritual walk as the disparity of wisdom was discussed to distinguish a particular standard of life. He declared, *"Now concerning the spiritual gifts, brethren, I would not want you to be ignorant or uninformed"* (1 Corinthians 12:1).

Paul explained that there is a measure of faith to all mankind. The believer who walks with the Lord Jesus Christ has received spiritual gifts. He described that the gift of God entailed a distinction of the Holy Spirit, and the wisdom of the natural man. Paul stated that when we pray and ask for the gift of God, there is an assurance that He is willing to grant His gift to the believer. The bible says, "God is no respecter of persons" (Roman 2:11).

In the book of Acts, the apostle Peter acknowledged that God is not prejudice concerning His gift as he testified in a similar verse that God is no respecter of persons (Acts 10:34). Peter had a personal encounter with the Lord as he was instructed to bless a Gentile family. Peter recognized that his ways were not God's ways, and the Lord had desired to bless Cornelius, and his family for his faithfulness towards God. The situation between Cornelius and Peter had highlighted the fact that the Lord dispenses great assistance of the Holy Spirit to anyone He desires. Here it should be mentioned that there is no preference with God, as the Lord does not consider academic achievements, the color of skin, or someone's status in life. The Word of God tells us that it gives God great pleasure to bless His people.

The apostle Paul stated that the Lord gives us gifts after the process of salvation; and these gifts and callings are irrevocable (Romans 11:29). The word "irrevocable" denotes "irreversible" and this means it cannot be denied or replaced. It confirms the type of God that loves us. It is important to mention how God in His wisdom makes no mistakes, for what He places within us He would never undo. The word of God tells us that the Lord sent His Holy Spirit to assist us to receive the gift of wisdom and revelation.

The Hebrew historians avowed that the Israelites had a verifiable amount of the wisdom of God from generation to generation. We read in the book of Genesis, the writer initially said that Noah was a righteous man who received wisdom from God to skillfully prepare an ark before the flood. Noah had to acquire the tools and dimensions to build an ark with much specification to house

INTRODUCTION

himself and family with all sorts of animals. There was a judgment pending for the earth and Noah received the divine intelligence. The parting of the Red Sea was a great miracle also. The bible also says that the Lord gave wisdom to Moses, and he led the people in the way of their deliverance. God instructed Moses to use the staff in his hand, and when he did the waters parted. According to the Sages, there was no room to turn or go forward at that juncture and the children of Israel were petrified. They say it was by faith that Joshua stepped into the sea and the water parted and they crossed over on dry land. Then, in the wilderness, God spoke to Moses again to prepare the people to meet with Him for them to receive revelation. As Moses climbed up the mountain, he also received revelation knowledge on how to build to the Tabernacle of God and the Ark of the Covenant to their exact specifications.

In reference to the facets of revelation knowledge, the Holy Spirit has a significant role in wisdom. One of the main functions of the Holy Spirit is to enable us to receive the gift of wisdom and revelation. Jewish History reveals that the success and victory of the Hebrew people was dependent on their obedience during their journey. They specified that whenever the Israelites sought the Lord God for counsel and forgiveness from disobedience, their spiritual wisdom and discernment was apparent to their performance. In addition, God gave them His divine guidance to journey in their lives, and He blessed them with godliness and prosperity for their obedience to His commands.

From Genesis to Revelation, there are details of the Lord blessing the prophets with wisdom. The prophets would admonish the people to seek the wisdom from God. In fact, the Lord desired to share His secrets with His people, and for them to have the wisdom that comes from God alone. There is an idiom that states that wisdom is a source of the honorable living, and this wisdom will develop a godly guidance. Thus, godly wisdom grows with the aged, and much understanding with length of days (Job 12:12). My prayer for you is that the Lord will grant a greater measure of wisdom and discernment towards the spiritual and natural things of God as you read this book.

Chapter 1
A Curiosity for Wisdom

"There is a path to Wisdom and Understanding."
(Proverbs 4:11)

One summer I decided to venture out to a recreational center with my boys. There was a camp event during that time for the kids and youths. The recreation facility had recently opened and there was an advertisement for the summer program for the neighborhood. It was scheduled for five days and there were several activities that were age appropriate. This was the first time that they would attend a summer camp, and they were eager to experience this.

When we arrived at the entrance of the facility, I observed there was a welcome sign posted for the camp in a huge gymnasium. It had a few arrows pointing in the direction leading to a lecture room. Following the arrows, we entered a dazzling lit room; its walls scenery attractively outlined the beach. There was art of a variety of seashells and sea creatures like sharks and whales. Besides, the floor tiles were of a hexagon shape layout and very attractive. Around the room were tables of a circular pattern, and each had six seats placement.

On the far corner of the room, there were a cluster of children, and the boys moved hurriedly towards the area where there were children lit up with cheerful smiles. As I averted to look in their direction, I recognized that there were some familiar faces who attended their regular school, and they were all excited. Suddenly, there was a sound of the rustling of a microphone, the atmosphere abruptly became silent. Our attention was drawn to an announcement that alerted everyone present that the program was about to begin in five minutes. Hearing the voice over the mic surprised them and their faces lit up with curiosity. Additional children entered the auditorium, and within a few minutes the program director stood up and introduced herself as Miss Kelly. Subsequently, she immediately began by offering a prayer to God for the success of the program. In that moment there was an eruption of chatter as they began to welcome the children.

The program leaders were then introduced, and she began to address the proceedings of the activities planned to the families. She detailed that on this first day; there would be an academic assessment to evaluate each child's need for tutoring. She advised the children that they were being tested for their proficiency in Math and Comprehension, and their task would require a progress report, to enable their success for the coming semester. She encouraged them to participate in all the other parts of their program, which she said, included tours, arts and crafts and drama. Soon after she explained the procedure, the children were directed to their assigned tables with nametags, and they were seated.

The children began to settle down as their individual math papers were distributed to them; a few more instructions were given. I watched as their characters began to shine as they began their task. I was now drawn to my inquisitiveness of the children's wisdom. I walked over to the director to get her permission to visit for a few more minutes. It was granted, and I took a corner seat away from the boys so that I can observe other children. There were two students seated on the table closest to me that seemed very efficient and skillful in their application to their assignment. Amazingly, these kids executed the answers in a few minutes on their papers. I watched as others took a little more time, but they finally solved their questions. At that point, there were some children that needed help, and they asked for assistance from their camp leaders.

I was astounded at their individual abilities, and I wanted to comprehend their wisdom. This experience stimulated my curiosity to understand the main concept of their natural ability to their reactions. I wondered why some children attained much more wisdom than others. I began to search for truth and the perspective of their ability to wisdom. From a scientific point of view the theory suggested that a child should begin at an early age to develop the basic principles of knowledge. They say that the source of their cultural morals could impact the accrual of their childhood; and their wisdom can be correlated to the reflection of their youth. Therefore, if the child is motivated with knowledge of the word of God, it would determine how they basically conduct themselves in different circumstances.

The following day the schedule was for an art and creativity class. I was eager to wait around, to observe what this class entailed. As we entered the room, the teacher had placed a variety of items for crafts in the center of each table. As they were seated, she invited the children to create any thing they desired, and that their art pieces would be exhibits at the end of the program. I positioned myself in the corner of the room to observe and not to distract the children. I recognized at the initial stage of the art session that there were several assorted papers, lollipop sticks, fabrics, and plastic bottles of glue. The children began to choose the items they wanted, and after a few minutes different products of creativity were on display at their table. As I gazed around the room, my eyes landed its focus upon a young boy that seemed physically challenged. He was seated at the far corner of a table, I had not seen him the day before, for he was conspicuous among the group. I was astonished at his skillfulness; his prominence in his talent capability was remarkable. He had selected the foil wrapping papers for his project and he began to crease and twist the papers. It began to take the formation of objects that resembled dinosaurs and birds. As I watched him, it triggered my imagination of what an intelligent boy he was, and in that moment, I recognized that his accomplishment was a manifestation of wisdom from above.

Still in the room, my gaze hastily turned to the table nearest the doorway, as there was an outburst at that table. I saw that there was a group of girls who were ecstatic over a very petite girl with blonde hair which led to an outbreak of applause. Her name was Aniyah, and she was dressed in a pink blouse. At that moment she was showing her friends the elongated hat that she had made. The simple fact that Aniyah took material to make a hat to match her pink blouse was stunning. She had formed a cone-shape out of a piece of white cardboard paper. She glued a variety of shapes from assorted pieces of glittering pink velvet. The trimmings of silver cord were quite astute to enhance her festive hat. The girls seeing that the cone hat that was upon her head was matching her fancy blouse is what initiated their hubbub. There were more surprises as other children made many fun items to display. They had transformed materials that were available into amazing things such as doll dresses, paper fans, telescopes, designed box cars and other gadgets which reflected their wisdom.

Now the evening of the final day of the camp was here and the families were reminded to attend the exhibition in the auditorium. The children's items were displayed on tables. Everyone gathered in the room when the Program director began to give a few students an opportunity to describe specific details of their exhibits. On one of the tables, there were displays of an assigned competition from a few students, who were now teens and had volunteered for the program. Miss Kelly announced that these students were challenged to use recycle products to recreate a new artefact for their display. Each of the teens had accomplished stunning items from the materials of their choice. It was mentioned that they recycled plastic bottles, cardboard boxes and pieces of fabric which was unrecognizable at a result.

The display of some toy dolls was the attraction for that evening. Many of the parents were gathering around this display with their children's curiosity. After a few proceedings, the director seemed enthusiastic to introduce to everyone the student who did the dolls design. She pointed towards a beautiful girl who was standing at the special project table. She introduced the girl as Gianna; and everyone began to take a closer look at her product. Miss Kelly began to coach her for the presentation while her parents began to prompt her with questions. With a shy demeanor, Gianna slowly began to explain her motivation for her design. She explained that the plastic bottles were her choice of recycle material and her inspiration to create dolls was to replicate the Barbie doll. We appreciated her astounding mission as she professed her desire was to present a doll to every girl that is not fortunate to obtain an original Barbie doll. Gianna acknowledged that her motivation was intended to put a smile upon every girl's face around the world.

After her speech, they showed a video of the process of her preparing the new product. It was remarkable to see her brilliance and technique, as she began to glue the yarn around the bottle structure in sequence. After a few attempts, she carefully filled the surface of the bottle until it was unrecognizable; this became the body feature for her doll. With a small Spiro foam ball, she used some glue to stick it to the bottle cover which created the resemblance of the head of the doll. Afterwards, Gianna artistically placed pieces of a velvet material to form the eyes, the mouth, and the nose, which materialized into the features of the doll's face. Subsequently, she used the pieces of hair that was in a basket and glued them upon the top of the Spiro foam ball; it made a wavy hairdo. At that point, she added a pair of plastic earrings that were attached to bobby-pins to enhance the face. The outline for the appearance of a female doll was convincing.

The woolly body of the doll was glued from the halfway point with a few layers of frilled lace to form their attire. At the top portion of the bottle there was a blouse designed to enhance the skirt. Her selection of glittery pieces of decor made the dolls really striking. The children were ecstatic, and their reaction had validated her product result. The dolls were an awesome transformation of some Gatorade bottles, and a few other products. This exhibit was undeniably one of the most remarkable pieces of art displayed at the tables. Instantaneously, there was an outburst of congratulations amongst the campers as Gianna finished her presentation. At that moment everyone proclaimed that this girl was a genius. Her project was a great achievement, and the Barbie dolls were amazing.

As I stood in admiration of her byproduct, I found myself pondering on the amount of time Gianna had to revise her idea.

It activated the opinions of the logical verified data of intelligence that a human can process. At the very moment, my interest shifted to the origin of wisdom, and how it affects every creature on the planet. This was evidence of Gianna's wisdom that seemed crystal clear. Somehow it propelled my thoughts to ponder on the different levels of knowledge. In the bible there are instrumental explanations of wisdom. It states the fact that at birth every child is given some measure of creativity. We read in the Word of God that God created the first man and He named him, "Adam." God gave him the gift of wisdom to name all the animals in the garden. Evidently, God also gave the animal kingdom some natural capability of intelligence. One animal, although vaguely mentioned, is the serpent. He, however, has great significance in scripture. The serpent spoke, and skillfully succeeded in tricking Adam and his wife Eve into committing sin (Genesis 3:1-6). In other cases, there are many animals which display actions beyond the natural habitations, and many animals are adaptable to their natural habitations, and the human comprehension.

Then, you read of stories that illuminate this principle of wisdom of people, who in their lifetime, have displayed talents beyond human comprehension. Scientists stated that an individual can achieve advancement in their life by investing in their development of wisdom. There is a grace upon every human life to operate in a natural gift of wisdom. In this respect, a human life can use their natural ability to accomplish the intellectual principles of wisdom. However, that wisdom can be used to our advantage or disadvantage, and it is advisable to be cognizant of this fact.

The word of God had specified the two classifications of the gift of wisdom. It had resolved that there was good and evil wisdom. The feature of wisdom in the book of Proverbs is the highpoint of this book. It has the spark of light that reveals what is stated concerning spiritual wisdom and the resolve of good and evil wisdom. Frequently, I was unresolved to a logical reason pertaining to the mystery of God, and how the human mind is ineffective. Such a curiosity stimulated my quest to comprehend wisdom regarding creation. This special gift of the wisdom of God is the elevating factor in our life pertaining to knowledge and insight which cannot be ignored. There are many facets to the topic of wisdom and the unexplainable knowledge has triggered my search to understand the profound and spiritual gift of wisdom from above.

Chapter 2
The Undeniable Wisdom!

All Glory to God!
It was early in the morning and outside was still dark when I was abruptly awakened. I heard a gentle voice, and I was consciously aware that it was His voice, as the Spirit of God began to speak. I was dumbfounded as I heard Him say, "The title of your book is *"Undeniable Wisdom."* I immediately sat up in the bed, and I refuted, "Lord, what do these words really mean?"

I had received other instructions before for my other books, but the Holy Spirit is so unpredictable and when you least expect Him to speak, He startles your understanding. I laid my manuscript aside for many months prior with a headline of "wisdom and understanding." I was uncertain of the appropriate title of the book. When suddenly, the Holy Spirit gave me the assurance I needed to confirm the name. He mentioned in such a gentle voice, that the words "Undeniable Wisdom" meant classified information. He impelled me that this title was intended to refer to something "Top Secret."

At an instant, it was revealed to me that this phrase symbolized a higher understanding, the knowledge that can only be activated through God's intervention. Immediately, in my thoughts there was a confirmation of an intelligence briefing. This was given entirely inspired by the Lord of the Hosts of angel armies.

As I sat up in bed, I began to research the CIA, concerning an "intelligence briefing." It states that the CIA is focused on the communication of the highest-level of intelligence analysis and is targeted at key national security issues and concerns. A president of a country and their highest-ranking military officers are privileged to receive this Intel on a regular basis. Hence, we can equate this knowledge to the privilege of receiving intelligence given to us from the Holy Spirit as a believer.

In the book of Jeremiah, the prophet declared that the revelations he received were absolutely from God. He described all his knowledge and experiences with God as nothing that was without the power of God. Jeremiah proclaimed that *"the whole world was established by the manifestation of God's Wisdom, and the sky was spread abroad by His Understanding* (Jeremiah 51:15). In one translation it says, *"He made the earth by His power; He founded the world by His wisdom and stretched out the heavens by His understanding"* (Jeremiah 10:12 NIV). He recognized that everything in his natural life had a connection to wisdom, even from the foundation of time.

In the word of God there was mention of a "Voice" in the beginning of time. The bible says that, even the cosmos was created by God's word and His glorious power in action. The entire world portrays the awesome scenery of the evidence of God's creation. There is no new entitlement or claim for mankind to suggest creation otherwise.

*"The Lord by **wisdom** founded the earth, by **understanding**, He established the heavens."*
(Proverbs 3:19 NKJV)

There are phenomenal signs which establishes the concept that portrays God as the Master Planner of all creation. The book of Genesis declares that in the beginning of time there was God the Father, God the Son and God the Holy Spirit. Divine wisdom is as undeniable as the existence of the Holy Spirit. The word of God confirms that the Holy Spirit was present beside the Father, as He spoke the worlds into being (Genesis 1:1). This theory speaks to the unified relationship of the "Trinity" in the process of creation. The bible illuminates the interaction of the Lord with wisdom, even before His works of old.

The persona of Wisdom spoke in the first-person point of view and proclaimed:

UNDENIABLE WISDOM

"I, Wisdom was with the Lord God when he began his work, long before he made anything else. I was created in the very beginning, even before the world began. I was born before there were oceans, or springs overflowing with water, before the hills were there, before the mountains were put in place. God had not made the earth or fields, not even the first dust of earth. I was there when God put the skies in place, when he stretched the horizon over the oceans. When he made the clouds above and put the deep underground springs in place. I was there when he ordered the sea not to go beyond the borders he set. I was there when he laid the earth's foundation. I was like a child by his side. I was delighted every day, enjoying his presence all the time, enjoying the whole world, and delighted with its people" (Proverbs 8:22-31NCV).

The undeniable evidence of the personality of God suggests that He is the One who imparts to the Holy Spirit, and then, the Spirit of God reveals the things of God to the believer. The Holy Spirit is known as the comforter, a teacher, and the revealer of all truth. The phase "all truth" is defined as being in accordance with fact or reality and truth is ascribed to things that are opposite of falsehood. The spiritual component of the Godhead is symbolized by the word "truth." The Holy Spirit resides within the heart of man and His presence serves to guide man through all spiritual insight relating to the will of God. His wisdom is for our life and wellbeing. The exceptional promise of God is to manifest through the fulfillment of His Holy Spirit within us. His primary purpose is to promote the divine power and wisdom of truth pertaining to God the Father and His son Jesus Christ. Therefore, a man cannot fathom the divine wisdom without the Spirit of God.

The scriptures make it known that the wisdom of God is His plan, from the books of Genesis to Revelation. As our father, God had created all things through His spoken word, for He is the great King who possesses all authority. After these decades, there is no mention of another being on the face of the earth that has ever articulated such words of supremacy. God is omniscient, and His persona consists of a third person perspective. The Apostle John declared, *"In the beginning was the Word, and the word was with God"* (John 1:1 NKJV). John stated that the Messiah "Jesus Christ" publicly declared that the wisdom He received was an undeniable gift from His father. Jesus said, *"The words I speak to you are spirit, and they are life"* (John 6:63 NKJV). In this phrase Jesus revealed that the words of God are unadulterated and authentic wisdom that discloses truth. The bible says that, in the beginning of creation, God the Father gave His son, "Yeshua," as the gift of salvation to the world.

A spiritual insight is revealed even before Adam fell. God planned for His covenant of love to cover Adam's sin with the shedding of blood. God knew that humanity would not recognize its inheritance of the Holy Spirit and so, He sent His son into the earth to convey His mercy and compassion. According to the bible, it was God's idea to freely distribute His divine gift of wisdom and discernment to those who seek the Lord Jesus Christ in sincerity. The words to "seek the Lord" can be referred to as an unpretentious surrender of our will to the Lord. His blessing of authentic wisdom is accessible through the declaration of our faith in Jesus Christ.

The prophet Amos confirmed God's covenant promises, that He would give divine wisdom to His faithful prophets (Amos 3:7). In God's covenant with Abraham, He promised there would be no withholding of secrets from His friend Abraham. God is still the same today, and He is no respecter of persons. According to Hebraic culture, they believe that God is undeniably a father who never shows favoritism. The scriptures say that *"Jesus is the same yesterday, today and forever."*

In the book of Acts, Peter reiterated that the Lord has no favorites, and this was revealed in the scenario with Peter and Cornelius. The Lord instructed Peter to bless the house of Cornelius with the Holy Spirit. However, Peter attempted to delay the blessings because of his own belief, but the Lord conferred to Peter that his conviction was irrelevant to His plan. The story specified that Peter witnessed the gentile, Cornelius and his family encounter the presence of God as they received the baptism of the Holy Ghost. In this story, Peter was cognizant of God, and his observation led him to repentance as he acknowledged that the Lord was no respecter of persons (Acts 10:34).

According to the book of Isaiah, the Father God will bless his people beyond natural abilities of knowledge or their undeniable wisdom. The prophet warned that the knowledge of God will guide the humble out of their phase of rebellion. Isaiah ensured that the priests who heard his warnings would enjoy the benefit of a supernatural gift of God. In another teaching, the apostle Paul declared that the believer would receive the gift of God through faith, and the experience of the supernatural (1 Corinthians 12:8-10). He reminded us of the love of God, that He has showered His people with His kindness in all wisdom and understanding.

The apostles noted that Jesus prayed on the mountain, and as He prayed His heart was full of compassion. Jesus asked His father to send the promise, the gift of the Holy Spirt, to the earth to abide within His people (John 16:5-7). In God's love for humanity, He desires to place in every person's heart a godly presence through the Holy Spirit. In Acts, chapter 2, as the Holy Ghost descended upon the believers in the upper room, the disciples experienced the presence of God and they testified that God's presence resided within their hearts. Undeniable wisdom is a gift from God, which is the spirit of wisdom and understanding, the spirit of counsel and strength, the spirit of knowledge and the fear and honor of God. These faith gifts are the benefits of God's wisdom and they are manifested in the areas of healings, miracles, discernment, prophecy, and the interpretation of tongues.

The bible says, Jesus spoke before his ascension and He requested that His apostles stay in the city. It was pertinent for them to stay in Jerusalem to wait for the power of the Holy Ghost. In other words, Jesus told them explicitly what would transpire when the Spirit of God comes upon them, that they would receive *"wisdom"* and the divine power to be able to be witnesses of God and demonstrate

His anointing. *"But you will receive power when the Holy Spirit comes upon you. And you will be my witnesses, telling people about me everywhere, in Jerusalem, throughout Judea, in Samaria, and to the ends of the earth"* (Acts 1:8 NLT). I submit that they received "the Principal Thing" as the Lord desired for His chosen people to walk in undeniable wisdom.

We can say that true wisdom is foremost a blessing from Elohim (God). As a believer the blessing of wisdom is not according to our name or our natural credentials. Neither is it according to our beauty or our assets. The principal of a Godly character is being wise and peaceful, it is of innocence and gentleness, it is of sincerity and lovingness, and it is being impartial to the extent of mercy and compassion.

The Lord is generally interested in our hearts' condition. God knows if our heart is pure and reverent towards Him. He looks at our principles to see if they are without any superficial elements of surprise. In this instance, the word "pure" could be used to describe a distinct quality of life in natural or spiritual logic. The spiritual definition of the word "pure" refers to a heart that is sincere, without malice, guiltless, and respects others, even in their sentiments.

The Divine Wisdom

The Messiah Jesus in His wisdom surrendered His will and became a living sacrifice out of His love for us. He left His divinity and came in the form of humanity to this earth to fulfill His Father's plan for redemption. He suffered and died on the cross, as the Lamb of God, for the whole world. The scripture say that He entered the belly of the earth to possess the keys of death and hell. After the third day, Jesus arose from the grave and was seen by men for forth days. Then, He ascended into the Heavens. Now He is seated on the right hand of the Father eternally, making intercessions for us (Romans 8:34).

There is a compassionate aspect to the spirit of God and the Holy Spirit accomplishes the will of the Father in the earth. As

Jesus walked upon the earth, the Spirit of God was instrumental in Him understanding the fulfillment of the divine commission of God the Father. Jesus Christ was raised from the dead through the power of the Holy Spirit. The Holy Spirit is also known as the Comforter or Helper. This same Holy Spirit has an awesome power of a warrior to be a protector and a defender, (likened as a Shield). King David, in his walk with wisdom, recognized that living in the presence of God would protect him from all harm (Psalm 35).

Jesus prayed to God on various occasions to send the Holy Spirit to stay within the disciples as divine wisdom. Jesus' desire was to have the presence of the Father dwelling in His followers as His Father resided in Him (John 17). Jesus said, *"My prayer is not for them alone. I pray also for those who will believe in me through their message, that all of them may be one, Father, just as you are in me and I am in you. May they also be in us so that the world may believe that you have sent me: I have given them the glory that you gave me. I have given them the glory that you gave me, that they may be one as we are one"* (John 17:20-22 NIV).

The scriptures tell us that Jesus in His wisdom healed those who were sick, and He set free those who were captives (Luke 4:18). He knew that the divine wisdom of God was instrumental in strengthening the disciples to be bold to teach and win souls for the kingdom of God. Even today, the Spirit of God is instrumental in guiding us how to successfully minister the Good News of Salvation. The Holy Spirit has the capacity to enable us to love like Jesus Christ loved, compassionately!

The Holy Spirit has a personality that activates the divine wisdom and knowledge of the truth of God in mankind. The Holy Spirit was there in the wilderness as the Israelites and Moses met at Mount Sanai, and we as believers, most of the time overlook their encounter with God. Moreover, on the day of Pentecost, the persona of the Holy Spirit was revealed again. The event was described as an appearance of a sudden rushing wind in the upper room where all the disciples were gathered. They had experienced the anointing of the Holy Spirit as it rested upon each of them

(Acts 2:2). The word, "sudden," could also be interpreted as without prior notice, abruptly, swiftly, or unexpectedly. The Spirit was illustrated by the words "rushing wind." This is a representation of God's awesome power. In Hebrew the word "Rauch" means the Holy Spirit of God, it is the representation of a breath or wind. Another way to describe it is likened to a gust or gasp. Therefore, at that moment, all the men and women that were present received an abrupt activation of the divine wisdom and power of God, and subsequently, they became inspired to do the work of the Lord with boldness and discernment. The apostle Paul explained that a believer's transformation process is initiated through the Holy Spirit (Ephesians 5:8).

The Spirit of God is the Spirit of divine wisdom, and His wisdom is longsuffering. The Spirit of wisdom usually amplifies the devises of the enemy and gives us the insight to heal the sick and the empowerment to set at liberty those that are in captivity of the oppressor (Matthew 10:1). Paul encouraged every believer to receive this gift of God to operate in the diversity of His revelation as it empowers the believer to discern truth.

The Sages recommend the studying of the word of God to result in an impartation of spiritual wisdom. They suggested that the believer should first take gradual steps towards growing in truth and wisdom in Jesus Christ. Their illustration was surrounded by the story of the Israelites' victory in relation to a convert or believer walking with the Lord. In the Book of Exodus, it tells us that God did not destroy the people of the land of Canaan instantly, but He drove them out little by little in His wisdom (Exodus 23:30). The Lord told Moses it would be too much, too fast, and the wild beast of the field would increase and occupy what they could not handle (Deuteronomy 7:22). It was to their advantage that God had not accomplished His promise too soon. This allowed their faith to increase as they conquered the lands. According to the Sages the believer's walk is to be of the same character as the wisdom of God and break down spiritual barriers with time as God did for the deliverance of Israel against all the nations.

UNDENIABLE WISDOM

In the Lord's conversation with Moses, He displayed wisdom as He spoke, *"Moreover, the LORD your GOD will send the hornet against them, until those who are left and hide themselves from you perish. You shall not dread them, for the LORD your GOD is in your midst, a great and awesome God. The LORD your GOD will clear away these nations before you little by little; you will not be able to put an end to them quickly, for the wild beasts would grow too numerous for you. But the LORD your GOD will deliver them before you and will throw them into great confusion until they are destroyed. He will deliver their kings into your hand so that you will make their name perish from under the heaven; no man will be able to stand before you until you have destroyed them* (Exodus 7:20-24 (NASB).

Even to this day, the inhabitants of Jerusalem could be seen as the Lord confirmed His plan to Joshua. He suggested that He did not want the children of Judah to drive out the Jebusites from Jerusalem but to dwell with them (Joshua 15:63). Jewish history describes these people as the tribe of Canaanites who were defeated by Joshua. They inhabited and built Jerusalem prior to the conquest by King David. The Hebrew word, "Jebus," means threshing-floor." They say that this was the place where the temple was finally built.

There is a story of a plague which caused the death of about 70,000 people in Israel and God commanded David to erect an altar. David went to seek a threshing-floor of a Jebusite named Araunah in the field of Mount Moriah in Jerusalem. The Sages stated that this was the very place that King David purchased, where he used the site of the threshing-floor to offer a sacrifice of repentance to God (1 Chronicles 21:24). Afterwards, David pleaded with God to end the vengeance and in humility, David asked for the angel of God to end the pestilence (2 Samuel 24:10-25). In God's divine wisdom, He showed how Israel possessed a portion of their land with a revelation of the bill of sale.

In the Israelite's battles God showed an awesome skillfulness and His undeniable wisdom. His preparation and provision for His people was instituted daily to recover all the lands. The lesson to take away here is that the plans of God for each person will take time and faith to believe that He is able to do what He said He will do and accomplish it in His divine wisdom.

Chapter 3
The Wisdom of Jesus Christ

The spirit of the LORD shall rest upon Him, the spirit of wisdom and understanding.
Isaiah 11:2 (NKJV)

The backdrop of Jewish history narrated the phenomena of Jesus' wisdom. The bible reveals that God is all-knowing; therefore, Jesus His only begotten son could be termed as a man full of wisdom. During Jesus' life He portrayed an enormous amount of wisdom and discernment. In some cases, Jesus used much restraint for He knew His ability, He was God in the flesh. He exercised wisdom in order to fulfill His purpose upon this earth.

Many theologians attempt to fill in those gaps for the childhood of Jesus; however, there is a lack of records regarding his growth and development stages. In the book of Luke, there is some revelation of a personal touch to His whereabouts. The canonical narrative concludes that Jesus was a Jew. As a child, He grew up in Judaism among the Galileans, and history recounts that that Jesus was amongst his siblings and his parents in His childhood until His teenage years. The Sages concede that Jesus' beginnings were in a poor and unschooled city. It was well perceived that the city of Nazareth was comprised of uneducated and poor people. The scholars of His day acknowledge this in their remarks concerning His city.

Mary as a gracious mother and as a Jewish woman may have had a great influence on her relation to Jesus. Most likely Jesus as a child would have mirrored her lifestyle. In the mere fact that Mary walked in godly wisdom, she had an encounter with an angel of God. She kept all her extraordinary encounters with the presence of God secret. History has no records to support that she revealed the prophecies of Jesus' life. As she pondered on the things the angel spoke concerning her son, the scriptures says that she hid it in her heart. Mary believed Jesus was the Messiah and prepared her son for his purpose upon the earth. The bible tells us that Mary followed Jesus on all His journeys and even to the cross.

Mary's Hebraic custom was to believe and adhere to all the words and commands that God instructed Moses. Her character of humility portrayed a righteous soul and her walk signified one who was in right standing with God. At the appearance of the angel of God, her reverence for God was proclaimed, and the angel honored Mary with the words, *"Blessed of God."* In her obedience to follow the Torah (The Scriptures), was the gift of divine wisdom and a special grace. Mary was rewarded as someone that was highly favored by God. The word "favored" in this text could be translated as highly recommended or referred to. When God chose Mary, He was making an allowance for His divine plan. He wanted her womb to be the vehicle of the miraculous birth of the Messiah and King, our Lord Jesus Christ. Throughout history, there is no woman likened to Mary.

Mary demonstrated knowledge of the greatest Commandment of God (Deuteronomy 6:4-6). God commanded the Israelites to love the Lord their God with all their hearts. In the Hebrew culture all children are encouraged to study God's statutes in order to obey Him. Therefore, their obedience required them to be passionate towards the things of God. As such, they are to keep His commandments by hiding/meditating on His word within their hearts.

The Sages advocated that the phrase "to obey" and "to do" were written separately to distinguish between two action verbs. They suggested that the action "to obey" meant that they had to learn the laws of God for themselves and comprehend what was required by the Lord. In addition, the phrase "to do" meant that all people are to practice what they preach. The Lord charged the children of Israel to teach these words or commands to their children, and their children's children. These instructions obviously require every generation present, and in the future to be taught the commandments of God. Evidently, Mary was knowledgeable of these commands and she obeyed them as she trusted God. Her faithfulness was acknowledged by the Angel and by being chosen as the one to bare the Messiah.

In the book of Luke, Chapter 2, Mary and Joseph in their obedience and reverence to the laws of God took baby Jesus to perform the covenant circumcision on the eighth day after His birth. The angel told Mary specifically that Jesus was His name, and He would carry greatness on the inside of Him, which was divine wisdom and discernment. This story revealed their belief in God and His covenant to the Jewish people. Even today, after centuries, the Jewish people customarily partake in ritual of the eight-day circumcision as God instructed Moses and the children of Israel.

In Hebrew, the act of circumcision is known as *"Brit Milah"* and all Jewish families understand the significance of participating in the covenant (Genesis 17:1-14). The removing of the foreskin was God's covenant promise made with Abraham and the children of Israel as a great sacrifice of love. The Sages accredited this act of circumcision as a sign of the blood covenant. In Hebrew the number eight is very significant as it symbolizes "a new beginning." In the word of God, Jesus Christ is referenced to the shedding of blood, as He was circumcised as a child, then, as an adult He offered His life as a sacrificial lamb. As the Messiah, He signifies the covenant pathway to salvation for the forgiveness of our sins.

A fundamental priority in the Hebraic culture is the teaching of the Word of God to children. Traditionally, this enriches their customs and desires to seek the wisdom of God. These principles of Judaism reveal that as a child Jesus' desire to be educated was substantial. The Apostle John said that Jesus participated in all the observances of their feast days and He prayed daily. Traditional Jewish culture is still found throughout many historical documentaries. The Jewish people still observe the seven days of Passover known as the Feast of Unleavened Bread, each year in Jerusalem. As their custom, all the families of Israel are commanded by the Lord to go up to Jerusalem to keep the Feast of Passover. At the event God commands the Priests and Levites to prepare the sacrifices and to give praise unto the Lord for all the great and miraculous things He has done for His people (2 Chronicles 30:21-13). This ceremonial custom is acknowledged as a memorial of their Exodus from Egypt. This is the illustration of our spiritual freedom and salvation from sin.

In another account of Jesus' ministry, John spoke of Jesus' discernment as He approached Phillip and called him to follow and become His disciple. The bible says that immediately Phillip in his wisdom went to find his brother and said that he had found the Messiah. Nathanael's cynicism was in response to his view of his hometown, that there would be nothing specular that would become of Nazareth; *"Can anything good come out of Nazareth?"* (John1:46 NKJV). Obviously, Phillip persuaded his brother to go meet Jesus. As Nathanael approached Jesus, the Lord called him by name, this made Nathanael express that Jesus was truly the Christ. The word "Christ" comes from the Greek word "Christos" which means "anointed one." The Hebrew translation of the word Christos is Messiah, and it means "one who is anointed."

The testimony of Jesus states that God anointed Yeshua, Jesus of Nazareth, with the Holy Ghost and with power. He went about doing good, healing all that were oppressed of the devil (Acts 10:38). There was an authentic level of wisdom and discernment in the supernatural nature of Jesus, for He accomplished various deliverances, healings, and restoration.

The apostle Paul proclaimed that there is a mystery of God. *"In whom are hid all the treasures of wisdom and knowledge"* (Colossians 2:3 KJV). The full mystery of God is: God as the Father, and Christ as our Lord are wrapped in divine wisdom and knowledge. As we receive Jesus Christ as our Lord and Savior there is a great anointing of the gift of wisdom that is found in Him.

The bible is full of descriptions of the life of Jesus Christ and His birth, He was shroud in divine wisdom that was inexplicable. The testaments of His disciples confirmed that the lifestyle of Jesus was of an observer of the law of the Torah (the Word of God).

THE WISDOM OF JESUS CHRIST

Whenever Jesus taught the people, He loved to highlight excerpts of the Prophets' writings. Jewish scholars say that Jesus frequently quoted the book of Deuteronomy more than any of the other books in the Torah. The Torah in Hebrew is referred to the first part of the Jewish Bible. It is the central and most documented history of Judaism and has been used by the Hebrews throughout the ages. It is in a sense, the most important reference of divine revelation to Israel and the Jewish people of God for teaching and guidance. King David admitted that the Lord had granted him with knowledge, but the source of his understanding was from the wisdom of God. *"I have more understanding than all my teachers. For your testimonies are my meditation"* (Psalm 119:99 NKJV).

The Lord's wisdom and knowledge cannot be bound by the wisdom of man. When the disciples asked Jesus which was the greatest of the commandments. Jesus in His wisdom responded by quoting Moses, "And you shall Love the LORD your God with all your heart" (Deuteronomy 6:5 NASB). Then, He said, "You shall love your neighbor as yourself" (Leviticus 19:18).

The Childhood Perception

Apostle Luke described Jesus Christ as a Jewish man in his writings. It appeared that Luke had firsthand information that placed him in the lineage of the priestly tribe. Luke was very familiar with all the priestly functions within the tabernacle and his records placed him within the vicinity of the Holy Place. Even though the bible never mentioned his connection to the tribe of Judah, Luke gave a detailed account of the Prophet Zachariah's location where he experienced the angel of God and it was Luke, the physician, who explicitly described the birth of John the Baptist and details of the event. Therefore, Luke had to be in close proximity to the tabernacle and godly men. In those days there were no Gentiles permitted to do the holy sacrifice to God, and no other tribe but the tribe of Judah.

During the time of Mary's encounter, there were no apostles mentioned in existence. Even after her encounter with the angel of God; Mary was afraid to share her experience with Joseph. The Lord Himself spoke to Joseph in a dream to reveal the conception of Jesus. The justification of Mary's pregnancy was private and unexplainable with no one present except the Holy Spirit. I submit that at Jesus Christ's birth, the only other human present was Joseph. The Bible tells us that Mary hid all these experiences in her heart. The Hebrew word for the name "Jesus" is "Yeshua" and it means "Salvation." Could it be that Mary never mentioned her experience with the angel of God to Luke? Perhaps, Jesus Himself revealed his dedication to the work of His Father to His disciples.

The apostle Luke gave great insight into the birth of Yeshua, Jesus Christ, more than any other texts. Mary would have personally told of her experiences with God to Luke (Luke 2:18-19). Luke's in-depth account showed lovingness towards Mary, which could have resulted in trust. His personal account from Mary's experiences with the Holy Ghost places him precisely in her circle. This information presents Luke as one that knew Mary's ventures through the birth of Jesus Christ and throughout His ministry (Luke 1:1-4). Maybe, Luke would have also been too young to know these things without Mary revealing them after Jesus began his ministry.

The Jewish history of the Sages suggest that the apostle Luke could have been Mary's physician, and this was the reason why she felt comfortable to share her miracle birth with him. There are some Jewish scholars who propose that in those days as they travelled with Jesus from city to city, Luke would have been their physician and I perceive that eventually Mary might have had the conversation with Luke. He became a follower of Jesus at the beginning of His ministry and Luke witnessed all the revelations including the death and resurrection of Jesus Christ.

God secured the miraculous plan of the birth of Jesus and the silence of His childhood for His survival. Mary raising a godly son was eminent and as a mother her character and influence equipped Jesus with Torah knowledge. Logically, Jesus and His family frequently attended the synagogue as their custom. His devotion to the word of God positioned Him to interact with their scholarly priest. The story of Jesus entering the Synagogue at the age of twelve years and asking questions boldly is mentioned.

In the scriptures there is mention of Jesus' depth of spiritual knowledge and discernment that caused surprise to others. They said, *"And Jesus increased in wisdom and stature and in favor with God and men"* (Luke 2:42 NKJV). The prophet Isaiah proclaimed that "The Spirit of wisdom and understanding, The Spirit of counsel and might, The Spirit of knowledge and of the fear of the LORD" was upon Messiah (Isaiah 11:2 NKJV) was upon the Messiah. Jesus increased in wisdom, and a reverential fear of God just as John publicized that the spirit of God rested upon Him. Jesus' reverence for the counselor of truth was shown in the word of God. His quality of being a unique young man brings a reflection of the child Samuel who stayed under the ministry of the priest Eli.

The Sages suggest that Jesus grew up around the carpentry industry. His earthly father, Joseph, owned a family business in carpentry (Mark 6:3). Some scholars purport that the authenticity of His development into manhood was spared from scrutiny. There was only one occasion the writer mentioned Jesus' age and it was while describing that Jesus and His family went to Jerusalem for the Feast of Passover. It is curious to envision that all the things' children love to do, Jesus must have enjoyed also, such as playing games, racing, and fishing. Moreover, Jesus was growing in a spiritual aspect as He and His siblings practiced their cultural customs under the influence and the protection of their parents.

The theologians were astounded at Jesus' awareness of the laws that were written in the scriptures. The bible says that they were amazed at His intelligence, as they often deliberated who Jesus really was (Luke 2:27). There are many theories that require exploring. In the Jewish commentaries there are some feasible explanations of this mystery concerning Jesus. Even today, theologians cannot fill in all the missing pieces of the untold stories of Jesus' childhood. They conclude that Jesus' life should be understood in comparison to a typical Jewish child and therefore, His life would entail all Jewish tradition.

On the Sabbath, all Jewish families, including their children, assemble in the Temple to be edified by the word of God. Their custom is to celebrate and spiritually elevate their children after they become twelve or thirteen years old. The child participates in an individual ceremony called the *"Bar mitzvah."* The word *"Bar mitzvah"* in Hebrew means, *"Son of Commandment."* It is a ceremonial representation of a boy or girl coming of age and their declaration for the first time publicly to "Teshuvah." This word in Hebrew is a verb which means "to turn" or "to return to God." The Hebrew word "teshuvah" is likened to the water baptism ceremony in Christianity. Following the occasion, the children become participants in all aspects of their Jewish religious expressions that should reflect their love of God's word and their faith to walk in integrity.

At this ceremony each child is given an opportunity to stand at the podium and read the Torah (The Word of God). Hebraic history mentions that boys most likely do this at the age of twelve while girls do it at thirteen. At this age, each teen commences their obligation to be accountable for their own actions and for their obedience to the commandments of the laws of God. Typically, as a teenager, it is clearly taught that it is their personal responsibility to read the scriptures for themselves. They are encouraged to seek the Lord for wisdom and understanding to walk in the fear of God.

In Judaism, a child is spiritually and physically connected to the Jewish Torah in appropriate developmental stages. They focus early on the writings of the Prophet Moses. The Jewish history states that in the Hebraic culture the Book of Leviticus is the first book that is introduced for reading to their children in the synagogue at the age of three to five years old. All Jewish children must begin their study of Torah to verbalize the laws at the age of ten years old. The Sages say that the book of Leviticus is predominantly known to the Jewish community as the emphasis of holiness and morals for living a sacred life before the Lord (Leviticus 17-26). This is astounding to Christians whose understanding is limited to their culture.

It seemed that Jesus was clearly in line with cultural customs, and it was the season for His Bar-mitzvah (twelve years of age), when He entered the Temple. Traditionally, it was a special time for Jesus, perhaps revealing the reason why the priest had allowed Him to have an opportunity to open the Holy Book and read the scriptures. I submit to the notion that Jesus would have memorized many scriptures in preparation. His attendance to the synagogue was each Sabbath with His siblings and the other Jewish children. Therefore, at the time of entering the temple, Jesus was very familiar with the teachings of the earlier Jewish Sages of Israel.

I remember one Sabbath, I watched a live broadcast of a Jewish boy's Bar-mitzvah. As I watched the proceedings, in the initiation of the celebration, the Rabbi introduced the young boy and congratulated him on his special day. Then, he was given the Tanakh which is the Jewish term for the written Old Testament. This youngster opened the scriptures to his choice for that moment (Isaiah 60:1-2). It was amazing to listen to the scriptures he chose that day as he began to recite these scriptures in the Hebrew language before he interpreted it into English. The young boy was bold, and he began to explain what the scriptures meant to him. This was important to him. Afterwards, his family came forward with a loving look of admiration and they congratulated their son. I reflected immediately on what it must have been like for Jesus, at the age of twelve, to do this very ceremony. In Jesus' presentation, He chose a passage scripture from the book of Isaiah which Matthew revealed was confirmation of the prophet's prophecy. The bible tells us that Jesus opened the book and proclaimed, "*The Spirit of the Lord is upon me, because he hath anointed me to preach the gospel to the poor; he hath sent me to heal the brokenhearted, to preach deliverance to the captives, and recovering sight to the blind, to set at liberty them that are bruised, to preach the acceptable year of the Lord*" (Luke 4:18-20 NJKV). Then Jesus closed the book, and gave it again to the minister and sat down. Afterwards, He began to say unto them, *"This day is this scripture is fulfilled in your hearing"* (Luke 4:21 NIV).

Mary's personality of faithfulness and reverence towards God could have been duplicated by other believers. In the fear of God, women and men could walk in the same manner, with their heart desiring to teach their children the fear of honoring God. This would result in the great reward of godly wisdom.

The Carpenter's Wisdom

Jesus Christ is the source of all knowledge, and His ability to build His Father's kingdom was evident. The apostle Paul stated that in Jesus Christ is hidden all the treasures of wisdom and knowledge (Colossians 2:3). The level of intelligence and discernment Jesus possessed in His lifetime upon the earth is unconceivable. The scripture tells us that Jesus Christ received the Spirit of His Father, and He was full of wisdom. This would suggest that Jesus functioned in wisdom beyond his years, in respect to the natural man. The mystery of God and our Lord Jesus Christ is divine wisdom. The word of God declared that the Messiah is Wisdom, and He is the beginning and the end of all things. The apostle John proclaimed that He is the son of God, He is the light to the world, and the Word of God (John 1:1). John the revelator spoke about a vision of the Lord and he called Him, "Yeshua ha Mashiach." This Hebraic name means that Jesus Christ was the "One" amongst the candlesticks. Jesus Christ is the same yesterday, today, and forever (Hebrew 13:8).

The Passover Feast is an eight-day festival that all Jewish people participate in. The significance of this season is for the Jews to celebrate their exodus from Egypt, and the mighty things that God has done for the children of Israel. Therefore, all the people would travel and gather in Jerusalem. The bible tells us that when the Passover Feast was over, it was time for the people to journey back home. Mary and Joseph were returning to Nazareth with Jesus and their family. After a few days journey, they assumed that

THE WISDOM OF JESUS CHRIST

Jesus was among the brethren's caravans when they realized that He was missing. So, Mary and Joseph began their journey in search of Jesus. It must have felt horrible to lose their young son, as they returned to Jerusalem to find Him. The account of John stated that it took them three days of searching before they found Jesus in the courts of the synagogue.

In that moment of Mary's bewilderment, she must have recalled the prophecy given to her about her child. Jesus was seated among the priest and the scholars of the word of God. She stared at Jesus as He was attentively listening to the preaching of their doctrine and as He undeniably displayed His wisdom and knowledge of the scriptures. Then, she heard Jesus ask some theological questions and the Hebrew scholars responded, but He came with another scriptural response. The bible says that they were quite amazed by Jesus and they recognized that He spoke as someone well educated while He opened the scriptures.

Luke 2:41-52 describes that when Jesus was at the age of twelve, he accompanied Mary and Joseph, and a large group of their relatives and friends to Jerusalem on pilgrimage, "according to the custom." There was no more mention of his whereabouts for many years until He appeared at John the Baptist's baptismal service. The Bible tells us that Jesus came near the riverbank of Jordan to be baptized (John 1:28). He was about thirty years of age (Luke 3:23). Jewish tales believe that Jesus had been involved with the family business of carpentry during those silent years. The Book of Hebrews describes God as the builder and maker. "Abraham looked for a city which hath a foundation, whose builder and maker is God" (Hebrew 11:10).

The Bible mentions the circumstances surrounding Jesus' birth and the escape travel from Israel to Egypt, then His return to Galilee, until the mentioning of His baptism. Afterwards, the beginning of His ministry became known. The theory of Jesus building things as a carpenter may have some relation to His desire to build the kingdom of God. Evidently, God Himself is a carpenter and the

Bible tells us that He gave Moses the instructions of how to build a pattern of His heavenly tabernacle on the earth.

Jesus' experience placed Him in the divine authority and power to begin His ministry. A greater presence of the anointing of God was upon Jesus when He returned to His hometown of Nazareth. Unfortunately, it became problematic for Jesus to minister there as His brethren rejected Him. The Sages say that Jesus' own brothers disregarded His gift and their skepticism limited Him from performing many miracles and deliverances among them. Therefore, Jesus went to Jerusalem and began His ministry as the attitude was propelling (John 1:11).

In the beginning of His ministry, Jesus was aligned with God's commands to fulfill the act of baptism. The Bible says that as Jesus approached John the Baptist for His baptism in the Jordan River, John bore witness that He was the Messiah. According to John, he saw the spirit of God rest upon Jesus, and he heard a voice from heaven saying, "This is my beloved Son, hear Him." Subsequently, Jesus was led by the Spirit into the wilderness where He stayed for forty days and forty nights, and there He was tempted by the Devil. In a similar passage of the Bible, it says that Moses, the prophet of God, was likened to the redeemer and deliverer. He went up to Mount Sanai and was there in the wilderness for forty days and forty nights in the presence of God and there he received great wisdom.

On the Sabbath, Jesus taught in the synagogue and they were astonished at His wisdom. Many of the priests inquired amongst themselves of the source of Jesus' wisdom for they were aware that Nazareth was not a place of higher learning. Jesus often addressed their Jewish traditions whenever they assembled; in those instances, He would rebuke the leaders of the synagogue for their man-made traditions. Jesus was knowledgeable of all their beliefs and His reproofs were explicit of their sinful state. He enlightened His followers of their traditions that were pertinent to their natural wisdom as He compared it to the wisdom that is from God. The Bible says that Jesus as the Messiah was acquainted with those priests who rejected the commands of God, and the rebellion of the people throughout their generations (Mark 7:7).

John tells us that the pessimists made their sarcastic remarks, because they identified Jesus as just Joseph the carpenter's son. They were limited in their understanding and seemed clueless of His wisdom, even though some saw His acts of miracles and naturally followed Him. His actions and speech caused them to question with whose authority His hands performed such miracles (Mark 6:2).

Apostle Luke declared that Jesus closed the book, and at that moment He proclaimed, *"This day is scripture fulfilled in your ears"* (Luke 4:18 KJV). Jesus' astuteness caused their eyes to be fixed on Him. The word "fixed" is a verb which explains their actions towards Jesus. It means, "to be fastened securely in a motionless position." These captivated theologians began to dialogue with Jesus, and He responded intellectually to their questions. Jesus' inquiry was astounding, an infinite wisdom that was expressed as the existence of the all-knowing God towards theology. Despite His critics, Jesus had the capability to build His kingdom. The accuracy of His title as the carpenter's son revealed that His wisdom goes beyond the natural understanding, for He is the rock of all fundamentals of natural and spiritual wisdom. The book of Hebrews states, "By faith Abraham obeyed when he was called to go out to the place which he would receive as an inheritance. And he went out, not knowing where he was going. "For he looked for a city which had foundations, whose builder and maker is God" (Hebrew 11:8 &10 NKJV).

Jesus was likened to a priest. He returned to Nazareth, and on the Sabbath day He entered the synagogue; Apostle Luke references this as His custom. At that time, Jesus had grown up, and they gave him the Torah to read the writing of the prophet Esaias (Isaiah). Immediately, Jesus opened the book where it was written: *"The Spirit of the Lord was upon m. Because the LORD has anointed me to preach good tidings to the poor. He has sent me to heal the broken hearted, to proclaim liberty to the captives, and the opening of the prison to those who are bound; to proclaim the acceptable year of the LORD, and the day of vengeance of our God; to comfort all who mourn"* (Isaiah 61:1-2 NKJV).

The Sages explained that every year, in the fall season, all the Jews celebrate their Jewish New Year which is known as "the Feast of Tabernacle" or "Sukkot." They say that the Jewish custom is to do a ceremony known as the "Water Libation" during the feast days. This tradition involves water as a source of life as God alone is the source of life and goodness. This custom consists of many priests, a lamp for lights, and water for cleansing (which they say is done to symbolize that "Yeshua" is our Salvation. He is the light of the world). They explain that during the fall season the priests would go down to the pool of Siloam, fill a golden vessel with water, and go up to the temple through the Water gate accompanied by the sound of the shofar and singing. They would pour the water so that it flowed over the altar along with wine in another bowl. This process is significant to the Jews prayer for the blessing of rain for their agricultural production along with the celebration of the Jewish New Year. In this tradition, all Jews felt obligated to participate regardless of their belief. The Apostle did mention that Jesus was in Jerusalem during this water liberation ceremony.

The apostle John gave an account of Jesus crying out at the last day of the feast. Jesus knew they understood the prophetic and, in His wisdom, He declared, *"If any man thirst, let him come unto me, and drink. He that believeth on me, as the scripture hath said, out of his belly shall flow rivers of living water"* (John 7:37-38 KJV). They were all present for the ceremony and they could hear His voice. The Sages say that Jesus was inviting them to be filled with the Holy Spirit. The Bible tells us that those who trusted in him, they would receive the Spirit later, for Jesus was not yet glorified. John indicated that of the people and priests who heard the words of Jesus, only some recognized that He was the Messiah. Again, they marveled at His words. The prophet Isaiah declared, *"Behold, God is my salvation. I will trust, and not be afraid, for the LORD God is my strength and my song, and He has become my salvation. Therefore, with joy you will draw water from the wells of salvation"* (Isaiah 12:2-3 NKJV).

John explained that the religious scholars began to query of each other what was said about their Jewish Messiah to come. They searched the scriptures to confirm if the prophets proclaimed that the Messiah would indeed come from Galilee. The Hebraic history stated, "The Messiah will come from David's descendants and from Bethlehem" (John 7:42 NIV). Their knowledge of the things of God was reputed as limited to the discernment of truth. Perhaps the priests and scholars of the word had an insufficiency of seeking the wisdom of God. In some cases, their obedience to the Lord could have revealed truth in secret.

Jesus revealed the scripture that confirmed who He really was to Israel and the world and they reacted in astonishment. In a Hebrew's commentaries, the Sages say that Jesus excluded the portion of the scripture "the Day of Vengeance." They indicated that the words omitted were about the last days, and it was not time for Jesus to return. The reference to the omitted words is mentioned by the John in the book of Revelation.

This topic of wisdom of the Lord God could go on without end. His word is centuries of years old, and it still stands to eternity. The full story of Jesus' wisdom is untold and those that were recorded, the Sages say are just a few so that mankind could comprehend what a mighty God He is.

Chapter 4
The Wisdom Phenomenon

"The fear of the Lord is the beginning of wisdom."
(Psalm 111:10 NKJV)

God is "all-knowing" and in Him all wisdom originates. The perplexity of all truth is the basis of wisdom. The Creator acquires all knowledge for eternity and there is nothing new God needs to attain regarding knowledge. Therefore, it would be accurate to propose that mankind has a limited access to knowledge.

The Bible is basically a book of wisdom and prophecy, consisting of supernatural guidelines to walking in the revelation knowledge of good success and health. God's word is vital to our wisdom and knowledge. The theological elements of wisdom describe that it operates in two components. The first component is that wisdom "tells us what to do," and the second is that wisdom "instructs you how to do it." The Bible admonished mankind to acquire wisdom.

True wisdom, according to the apostle James, is essential to all revelation that is received from the Father which is in Heaven. The apostle encouraged all believers to ask the Lord for divine wisdom. The scripture says, "Happy is the man who finds wisdom, and the man that gain understanding" (Proverbs 3:13 NKJV). The Passion translation stated, "God's Blessings pour over the one who find wisdom." Therefore, James suggested that if anyone lacks wisdom, they should ask it from God (James 1:5). James attested that God will generously give us wisdom without finding fault or disapproval.

Wisdom symbolizes several facets of God; James explained that it is first pure and authentic. The Bible says, "Wisdom that comes from heaven is first pure, then peace-loving, considerate, submissive, full of mercy and good fruits, impartial and sincere" (James 3:17 NIV). The word "pure" can be defined as "not mixed or adulterated with any other substance or material." The word "peace-loving" can be termed as "free from disturbance," or "tranquil and calm." The term "considerate" is defined as "having or showing a mild, kind, or tender temperament or character, moderate in action not harsh." The word "submissive" means "to give way under pressure, not hard or rigid." The term "full of mercy" is likened to "compassionate, empathy, having a capacity to forgive, or showing kindness." I could go on, but these are some characteristics of a loving God. The spirit of wisdom is the character of God. Wisdom can still be defined in other ways, as it leads us to be pure, friendly, gentle, kind, helpful, genuine, and sincere.

The English definition for the word *wisdom* is *"the quality of having an experience, or clarification of knowledge, and a virtuous judgment"* (dictionary.com). Therefore, wisdom is a virtue or a state of being. In this case, wisdom has a resolution and can be equated to the laws of God. Thus, natural wisdom is a quality for the advanced developmental state of a person that relies on extraordinary knowledge and understanding. Moreover, genuine wisdom could be the discernment of moral values by way of right judgment and insight regarding a perspective or interpretation intended for courageous actions.

The probability of the truth of God's wisdom transcends the perspective of a human thought. The psalmist David declared that the phenomenon of wisdom is the law of God. In his point of view, David articulates "The law of the Lord is perfect, converting of the soul" (Psalm 19:7 NKJV). He conferred that the law is the testimony of the Lord, and it was guaranteed to make the humble prudent or wise. The intellect of mankind is identified by the evidence of their understanding, though there is a notable difference between the words wisdom and understanding.

The dictionary definition for the word understanding is "the ability to comprehend things; or to have an insight of things" (dictionary.com). Thus, it differentiates the word understanding from the word wisdom. For example, wisdom means having qualities to be compassionate, sympathetic, considerate, patient, merciful, forgiving and longsuffering.

In theological logic, the word "wisdom" is defined as *"an ability to judge correctly"* which is based on the knowledge and understanding of God's word. A theologian stated, "true wisdom is consistent with a reverence towards God as our Creator, along with the respect for all people". Therefore, spiritual wisdom causes someone to have coherence to truth regarding humanity. Subsequently, wisdom consists of a heavenly blessing that is morally untainted.

The gift of God is acquiescent to the wisdom of God as the function of the gift is embodied in spiritual wisdom. Spiritual wisdom is defined as *"the ability to discern and differentiate, or judge those things that determine what is true, what is right and what is lasting or eternal."* The effective part of revelation is wisdom and spiritual discernment through prayer. It consists of a variation of God's divine work that leads to healing, deliverance, and many other supernatural miracles. There must be fervent prayer and the reading of God's word to acquire spiritual wisdom and, to activate His promise of wisdom and glory.

There is great insight regarding Godly fear as the Psalmist David gave a firsthand example of the fear of the Lord as the beginning of wisdom. In the Hebrew language the word "fear" is attributed to a type of reverence and respect towards God. In the Bible, the word "fear" was used about 70 times. The fear of the Lord is prioritized as the principal thing and it relates to a reverential basis of humility and honor of the judgment of God. The acknowledgment of God as the creator of the universe and as the Supreme Being deserves godly fear and respect. King David received wisdom for he understood that the testimonies of God were established forever (Psalm 119:152). He pursued the knowledge of the word of God, and he sought directions from the Lord.

The apostle Luke stated that Jesus declared, *"Truly I tell you, this generation will certainly not pass away until all these things have happened. Heaven and earth will pass away, but my words will never pass away"* (Luke 21:32-33 NIV). Moreover, Jesus declared that it would be easier for Heaven and Earth to perish, than for one word or tittle of God's law to fail or "miss the mark".

The Wisdom Gift

"But the wisdom that is from above is first pure, then peaceable, gentle, and easy to be intreated, full of mercy, and good fruits, without partiality, and without hypocrisy. And the fruit of righteousness is sown in peace of them that make peace."
(James3:17-18 KJV)

Wisdom is the first mentioned of seven gifts of manifestation of God's spirit. The characteristic of the foundation of wisdom consists of an eternal nature that is complete or unpolluted. These heavenly gifts are distinctly different from the *fruit* of the Spirit. The seven pillars of foundation were envisioned by John as he saw the seven candle sticks on the Menorah (Revelation 1:12).

The fruits of the spirit are the reflections of the seven branches of the tree in Revelation. The meaning of the word "fruit" can be reference to the word *"ovary."* The Sages liken the Spirit of wisdom to the innocence of a virgin and its purity is incomprehensible. Moreover, the fruits of the spirit are the godly wisdom that includes gentleness, peace, loving, mercy, sincerity, consideration, reasonability, impartiality, and submissiveness. They conclude that godly wisdom is creative, and it has a willingness to readily serve others. A Hebrew commentary explained that godly wisdom is never conflicting and doesn't participate in dispute for there is never a display of favoritism.

There are a few replications of the gift of wisdom that are written in the book of Exodus. There is an exceptional story of Moses, the servant of God, who desired for the Lord to make His ways know to him. The scripture states that God revealed attributes of His persona to Moses, as he saw God as a merciful and compassionate god. Moses' affiliation with the power of God resulted in the evidence of wisdom and maturity. By faith, Moses believed that

THE WISDOM PHENOMENON

God is a promise keeper. His compliance to speak to the children of Israel about God's commands demonstrated that he literally and continually heard from the Lord. The fact that Moses had the capability to convey the messages of God and communicate back to God what the people responded was the gift of wisdom.

The Israelites primary success was their obedience towards God's command that He would bless His people with the richness of the gift of wisdom for all the nations. Therefore, the children of Israel were instructed to cleave to the Lord with all their heart and soul (Deuteronomy 4:5-6). Their retort to His command was for them to seek godly wisdom and morals purposefully. The Hebrew Sages say that the first word mentioned in the phrase of His command was to love with all their heart. It was the revelation of the key to love and the importance of the heart that was pointed out before the soul. The ultimate action was first to love God, then to love people. Moses instructed the children of God to *"cleave,"* this action is intended to be distinct, "to cleave" is equated to a child clinging to its mother. Moses explained that these two ordinances require a persistence of doing and keeping in respect to attaining wisdom.

God chose the people of Israel to be a beam of light to the nations. Their peculiarity was noticeably their divine wisdom, and this would be recognized by the nations. God's plan was inclusive of the wisdom for the Israelites spiritual welfare and their civilization, to equip them to be counselors to the nations in their conversion towards the Lord.

In Hebraic history they say that the wisest king of all times was King Solomon. The Bible tells us that Solomon prayed to the Lord and asked Him for wisdom to guide him in the kingship after his father David died. God displayed His preference rewarding Solomon with the gift of wisdom, beyond his years because Solomon didn't ask for material possessions but spiritual discernment. Jewish history reveals that Solomon gave great counsel to the people of Israel throughout his kingship. They tell the example of the Queen of Sheba who journeyed for several miles to Jerusalem, to see the king Solomon. The story noted that she wanted to test him and to hear his counsel (2 Chronicles 9). The queen in her skepticism came to understand if it was possible for the king's reputation to be distinguished with such wisdom.

The Sages say that Solomon was full of wisdom and he acknowledged his errors. Solomon wrote an assurance to Israel saying, *"My people are destroyed for lack of knowledge"* (Hosea 4:6 KJV). Before the end of his day king Solomon penned a variety of sayings concerning wisdom intentionally to give insight to the people of Israel of how to achieve faithfulness towards the Lord. He had begun to disobey God during his kingship in pride and arrogance. Solomon entangled himself with pharaoh's daughter and he continually married other heathen women against God's command. The Sages say that he did this for political association in business, to acquire materials for the Temple construction. Moreover, to appease his wives, Solomon began to worship their gods. This was an abomination to God and Solomon's kingdom was judged. I submit that wisdom could be abused, as pride puffs up in wisdom.

Wisdom can be described as a dynamic function in life under the jurisdiction of God. The world operates in time and seasons which are all within the hand of God and will ever cease according to (Genesis 8:22). The psalmist David declared that his times were in the hand of God (Psalm 31:15). He was accrediting God for the protection he experienced from his enemies. David totally trusted in God as he was riddled with challenges. He understood that in the secret place of God's presence was his shelter, and in His presence was the counsel of the gift of wisdom he needed to endure in times of trouble.

> *"For the LORD gives wisdom, from His mouth come knowledge and understanding"*
> (Proverbs 2:7NKJV)

THE WISDOM PHENOMENON

In the book of Corinthians, the apostle Paul explains the gift of God as a divine gift (1 Corinthians 12:8). Paul explained that spiritual wisdom is manifested in every believer to profit the body of Christ. There are seven gifts of God known as the word of wisdom, the word of knowledge, faith, the gift of healing, the working of miracles, the gift of prophecy, diverse kind of tongues, the interpretation of tongues, and the discerning of spirits. Specifically, the gift that was mentioned immediately after the word of wisdom was "knowledge." The word "knowledge" can also be associated with the ability to teach another person with a form of revelation in faith. According to the prophet Isaiah the Lord Jesus Christ operated in the gift of God. This divine gift is available to all believers.

In the book of Hosea, he warned the nation of Israel that their destruction was a result of the limited knowledge and faith towards God. Hosea 4:6 says, "God's people are destroyed for the lack of knowledge." The children of Israel were given the law, and the promises of God. They were to believe in their coming Messiah who would save them from their sin. However, they did not take heed to the wisdom of the prophets and God's caution about having an understanding to avoid the consequences of their disobedience.

Hebrew theologians recommend that the people who put their trust in the Lord Jesus Christ do definitely mature in wisdom. They encourage believers of the faith to study the word of God, as it would influence an untainted innocence toward the love of the Lord.

Chapter 5

The Foundation of Wisdom

"The LORD brought me (Wisdom) forth as the first of his works, before his deeds of old: I was formed long ages ago, at the very beginning, when the world came to be."
(Proverbs 8:22-23 NIV)

The Word of God tells us, "In the beginning, God!" (Genesis 1: 1 ESV). This phrase was also referenced by the apostle John, *"In the beginning was the Word, and the Word was with God, and the Word was God"*—*"wisdom"* (John 1:1-2 NKJV). According to the scripture the Godhead is the Trinity who consists of God the Father, and the Son, and the Holy Spirit. The Trinity was all intricate in creation of the foundation of life. According to His word, in His completeness is wisdom and the foundation of the earth manifested in the presence of God the Father.

God was in covenant with the Holy Spirit in the beginning of the world. The Holy Spirit is referenced as the custodian of wisdom, He reveals that the spirit of God has a substantial knowledge of the accessibility to the wisdom of God. I will acquiesce that in the beginning of time, the Holy Spirit had the secrets of all spiritual wealth and all-natural wealth. This confirms that the wisdom of the Holy Spirit is the pioneer to enforce wealth in our lives.

In the book of Genesis, we read that *wisdom* was present before the formation of the earth, and that it was the source of the creation of mankind and every living creature. In another revelation it is mentioned that God is light. This shows that, wisdom created the light in the beginning, when there was gross darkness upon the earth. Furthermore, God in His wisdom came as the Messiah of the world in the form of humanity, and John the apostle proclaimed, "Jesus Christ is *the Light of the world*" (John 8:12 NKJV). John referred to the people as walking in darkness until they had seen the light. Jesus Christ came into the world and He gives light to the world through His salvation.

UNDENIABLE WISDOM

John's personality reveals that he was very observant towards details; he noted that Jesus during the ministry walked in great wisdom and discernment. In John's writings, he narrated that whenever the disciples questioned Jesus, His response was profound. Once Jesus answered and said, *"If a man loves me, he will keep my words: and my Father will love him, and We will come unto him; and abode with him"* (John 14:23 KJV). Jesus was explicit in saying that the divine presence of God would dwell within their hearts. This is confirmation that the gift of the spirit of God will abide within the believer for them to have the ability to walk in spiritual wisdom and discernment.

The book of Proverbs has a substantial number of idioms pertaining to wisdom. The writer pointed out that the foundation of wisdom was an affiliation with God in the heaven. The scripture tells us, "Wisdom was there as the heavens were prepared, and when He set a compass upon the face of the depth." In this phrase, it affirms that wisdom dwells in the presence of the joyful father of creation. In this phrase, wisdom presented an intimacy with God: *"I was constantly at His side, I was filled with delight day after day, rejoicing always in His presence"* (Proverbs 8:30 NIV). Wisdom also reveals its personality in the relevance to the Father of all creation saying, *"I (wisdom) was born when there were no seas, when there were no pools full of water. I was born before the mountains and hills were in their places. It was before He had made the earth or the fields, or the first dust of the world"* (Proverbs 8:24-29 NLT).

Wisdom completely functions by the Holy Spirit, and by the power of God the Father and His son, Jesus Christ. The Spirit reveals who the Lord Jesus Christ is through spiritual wisdom. The scripture says that the spirit of God is the source of all godly wisdom for He will guide us in *all* truth (John 16:13 NKJV). Therefore, spiritual wisdom requires diligence in reading the word of God and a willingness to seek the Lord by spending time with Him to teach us revelation and truth.

The Lord commanded every child of God to desire the wisdom of God in their lifetime. As the children of God were in rebellion

THE FOUNDATION OF WISDOM

against the Lord, the prophet Hosea penned these words about their disobedience towards the wisdom and knowledge of the power of His word. What is the knowledge God is speaking about? The answer to the question is the obedience of understanding and reading the Word of God. God specifically told the prophet Hosea the condition of the heart of His people. He declared, *"My people are destroyed because of a lack of knowledge. Because you have rejected knowledge,* I will also reject you from being priest for me; because you have forgotten the law of God" (Hosea 4:6 NKJV).

An enlightening theory stated that the intelligence of children and their mannerisms could be reflected by of the level of wisdom introduced in the home. The impact of parental influence can effectively be reflected as the child individually displays their point of view. This theory relates to their natural wisdom towards spiritual things, this is in respect to their parent's initiation of the word of God in that home. They display of spiritual life that portray a diversity of facets in the children instinctiveness, creativity, and educational wisdom. In some cases, the children can exercise counsel that could be potentially enhanced by their spiritual wisdom; that is astounding to them in the operational skills of life.

The Mystery of Wisdom

"The spirit of the Lord shall rest upon him, the spirit of wisdom and understanding, the spirit of counsel and might, the spirit of knowledge and of the fear of the LORD."
(Isaiah 11:2 KJV)

The Holy Spirit functions to give illumination to the mystery of wisdom and understanding. On this subject, the scripture tells us that the spirit of God is the origin of the mystery of wisdom. This subject is discussed in another chapter that states that the mystery of wisdom is referred to a specific gender. The word of God proclaimed that there is the personality of God, which is the Father, the Son, and the Holy Spirit. The Prophet Isaiah proclaimed that there are seven manifestations that took place when the spirit of God rested upon our Messiah, Jesus Christ. There is the spirit of wisdom, the spirit of understanding, the spirit of counsel, the spirit of power (might and strength), the spirit of knowledge (discernment), and the spirit of the fear of the Lord (the spirit of reverence and honor for God).

The Hebrew Historians commentary highlights that the word *"wisdom"* was written 344 times in the scriptures and the word *"understanding"* was mentioned 91 times. In the beginning of the book of Proverbs was the first mention of the word wisdom, and the scripture specifies, *"Wisdom is the principal thing; therefore get wisdom: and with all your getting, get understanding"* (Proverbs 4:7 KJV). Another translation says, "The beginning of wisdom is: acquire wisdom; and with all your possessions, acquires understanding" (NASB). The mystery of wisdom is simply to obtain knowledge. The mystery of wisdom was also interpreted as, "God is here!" His wisdom is here calling to us, and He wants us to know Him. This idiom is an invitation to spiritual wisdom of the perception of God.

The secret of salvation is found in the mystery of God. This statement illuminates the fact that mankind cannot achieve wisdom on their own merit. It is only a supernatural working of God and He alone determines the magnitude of the wisdom anyone can attains. According to the apostle Paul there is a mystery of God that is designed and hidden in the wisdom of His glory from the beginning of time (1 Corinthians 2:7). Paul acknowledged that there is only "One" that can reveal the truth and He is our Lord God.

The first and most prominent sentence of Jesus' prayer is for His followers to know the Father, and then, to know Jesus Christ His son. The apostle John stated that Jesus said to his disciples and the Jews who believed in him; that they must continue in His word. These phases were likely to encourage them to persistently learn the spiritual aspects of God's nature to grow and increase in wisdom and understanding (John 17:3). However, our natural

THE FOUNDATION OF WISDOM

mind is ill-equipped to determine the whereabouts of spiritual and natural wisdom.

King David penned a significant notion to describe wisdom saying, *"Wisdom and understanding was first placed in the inner parts of all God's creation"* (Psalm 51:6). David declared that the principle of God's word and the knowledge of truth hinges on divine wisdom. In the Book of Deuteronomy as Moses anointed him to take his place, the prophet Joshua was given the key to wisdom. Moses cautioned him to be steadfast in studying and doing all that was written in the word of God, for it would be beneficial to his wealth and good success (Joshua 1:8). The believer's key is to study diligently and meditate on God's word.

The scripture declares that as Moses rehearsed the journeys the Israelites experienced; he began to remind them in their advancement to possess the land of Canaan; it required trusting God for His wisdom. Moses cautions the children of Israel to be steadfast, and to cleave unto the Lord God, for in this all their life ventures would be fulfilment. Their livelihood was dependent upon their people keeping and obeying all of God's commands (Deuteronomy 4:4-6). Their example is essential for the believer not to forsake God and His word, to benefit and to grow in the wisdom of God (Proverbs 4:5). This suggestion reveals that wisdom is a process that increases with time.

> *"This book of the Law (God's word) shall not depart out of thy mouth, but thou shalt mediate therein day and night, that thou mayest observe to do according to all that is written therein: for then thou shall make your way prosperous, and then thou shall have good success."*
> (Joshua 1:8 KJV)

The mystery of the Holy Spirit today was the very glory of God in the days of Moses. The Sages say that throughout the scriptures there are mysteries, and one significant mystery was that of the rock that followed the children of Israel as they journeyed through the wilderness. This rock in the wilderness was the identical rock that Moses struck to get water. The scripture declares, Jesus Christ is that spiritual Rock of our salvation. In his writings the apostle Paul mentioned the mystery of wisdom. He proclaimed to his brethren that they should reminisce on the rock; for that rock was God, who did preform many miracles for their ancestors. The forefathers experienced that rock as they drank the spiritual water, and they ate manna (their spiritual food sent from the heaven).

It was Paul who made referred to the wisdom of God as the divine revelation of the nature of God. Paul stated, *"For what man knows the things of a man, except, the spirit of the man which is in him?"* Paul added, *"even so no one knows the things of God except the spirit of God"* (1 Corinthians 2:11-1 NKJV). The proclamation of the mysteries was that all the hidden things of God were predestined before the foundation of the world unto the glory of God which abides in us. The Jewish Sages stated that it is only through the wisdom of God that an individual is lead to salvation and redemption by the power of the Holy Spirit to receive righteousness and sanctification. This phrase affirms that the mystery of God's wisdom is required for a relationship with the Lord Jesus Christ, to obtain spiritual knowledge of the things of God.

An intricate function of the personality of wisdom is in the divine power of holiness and morality of the believer, as wisdom aids to accomplish their destiny. According to the book of Leviticus, the spirit of wisdom also intervenes in matters of civil and governmental affairs of the world. The Bible states that wisdom is a guideline for insight to the knowledge of counsel for men and kings. One scholar stated that there is no wise counsel apart from God and His word for they are one. The Bible declares, "Where there is no counsel (wisdom) the people fall, but in a multitude of counselors there is safety" (Proverbs 11:14). The Spirit aids our discernment and reverence towards the spiritual boundaries that the Lord has established for our protection. The apostle Paul encouraged Timothy to mature in wisdom and in the knowledge

THE FOUNDATION OF WISDOM

of God (1 Timothy 2:4). His advice implied that Timothy's success would depend on his desire for spiritual wisdom. For Timothy to be equipped for God's kingdom building it would involve the knowledge of the word of God.

The Means of Godliness

The affluence of godliness is a function of the Holy Spirit to create the wisdom of God. The prophet Isaiah affirmed that it is the spirit of God who guides the Son in all His counsel and instructed Him in the ways of understanding (Isaiah 40:10-14). The scripture tells us that Jesus operated in wisdom and He acknowledged that only what His Father instructed Him to do, He could do (John 5:19). Therefore, God is Holy, and Jesus is the reflection of His Father.

The gift of wisdom intertwines to achieve the spiritual and physical aspects of life concerning integrity and holiness. This dynamic godly wisdom can result in the reverence towards God's sovereignty and to the observance of His laws. Scripture tells us, "Without holiness we shall not see God" (Hebrews 12:14). It is God's desire that all men walk in wisdom and devotion to Him. There are many scriptures that illustrate the function of wisdom in men and women of God.

Godliness is a reverence for God and a life of holiness portrayed in this world. This lifestyle results in manifold blessings that lead to revelation knowledge and spiritual discernment. The apostle John affirms that wisdom is a spirit that resides within you. Hence, the spirit of godliness resides within our hearts to help us not to sin against God. Therefore, the spirit of wisdom is the spirit of truth that is associated to the supernatural understanding of faith (I John 5:6). Paul, the apostle, prayed for the saints that they would be filled with the knowledge of God (Colossians 1:15). The word "fill" suggests that the quality of divine wisdom is attained to know God personally and to understand His attributes as our Lord. This is determined by the process of seeking the Lord in prayer and reading of His word. To a believer, it is advantageous to cultivate a virtuous character of the holiness of God through Salvation.

There is another teachable moment in this scripture where David declares, *"The mouth of the righteous speaks wisdom and his tongue talks of the justice"* (Psalm 37:30 NKJV). This statement can also be read as "the godly ones could offer good counsel because, they are teachers of right from wrong." The experiences that David personally had with the God of Abraham, Isaac, and Jacob made him mindful of his choices. David emphasized that he set the Lord before his senses or his own wisdom for it was the only path to real godliness and blessings. In seeking the wisdom of God, the Bible tells us that David received the divine justice of God (Psalms 16:8).

Moreover, Daniel received the vision of those who are godly, and they were full of wisdom to discern the things of God. He declared that they would shine like the brightness of Heaven's dome, and they will turn many hearts to righteousness as the stars forever (Daniel 12:3). The word "turn" in this phrase means "to convert hearts towards the Lord." The word "dome" references an atmosphere of a filament-like structure or a vast ceiling that is likened to a roof.

Chapter 6
Wisdom Likened to a Woman!

"Unto you, O men, I call; and my voice is to the sons of man."
(Proverbs 8:4 KJV)

In the Hebrew language, the word description that God used for a woman was "Ezer." In Genesis 2:18 God said, *"It is not good that man should be alone; I will make him a helper"* (NKJV). The word, "Ezer," is in the form of feminine gender for wisdom. It means *"to help or a helper."* The woman is designed to be an *"ezer"* or a "helper" to the man. Eve's name in Hebrew means "life or a source of life" (Genesis 1:27).

Hebraic history associated God's creation of the first woman named Eve to the word "wisdom." The Sages believe that God created Eve to be a helper for Adam. There are scriptures in the Old Testament that uses the word *"ezer"* (wisdom) in reference to God as our "Helper" in Hebrew. In the English Bible, the word "ezer" was written as a character of Yahweh (YHVH) or God.

Wisdom is a depiction of a gender role in the Hebrew language. In the beginning of creation, there was unification of the Holy Spirit and God the Father. Hebrew scholars refer to wisdom as the feminine part of God's nature of nurturing and empathy. The personality of the Holy Spirit is a representation of valor, strength, and might. The "Proverbs 31 woman" gives the text personality, and context to wisdom.

According to the Hebrew Sages commentary, the Book of Proverbs ultimately reveals that someone was beside God, as the master workman (Proverbs 8:22-31). The phrase did not indicate what the relationship was, or the status of the other entity involved. However, the word *"helper"* implies that there was someone that provided aid or amenity.

The Gematria aspect of the word "ezer" demonstrates the basics of the Hebrew alphabet that comprise Hebrew letters, and their numerical value. The word "ezer" has a numeric value, and its letter components spell out the words as "ayin, zayim and resh." The simple order of explanation is as follows:

- Ayin - represents the eye and means "to see" or "to experience." It has a numerical value of 70.
- Zayim - represents a weapon such as a sword or a plow and means "to cut off." It has a numeric value of 7.
- Resh - represents a head person, or "the first." It has a numerical value 200.
- Therefore, the total numeric value for *"Ezer"* is 277.
- In Hebrew, the number 270 represents the word: "Peacemaker"

The phrase in Hebrew for a peacemaker has similarity to the word "wisdom." In fact it is the exact meaning for the word "helpmate" and "protector" (likened to a woman or a wife). There are a few scriptures that refer to "the Helper" that can relate to the Lord our God.

For instance, *"Behold, God is my helper; the Lord is the sustainer of my soul"* (Psalms 54:4 NASB). In the book of John, Jesus proclaimed, *"the Helper, the Holy Spirit, whom the Father will send in my name, He will teach you all things, and remind you all that I said to you"* (John 14:26 NASB). In other words, Jesus was confirming that the Holy Spirit is the Spirit of wisdom and truth.

Idioms are written in the bible as illumination of the character of wisdom as a woman. It states that, *"Wisdom calls aloud outside; and she raises her voice in the open squares"* (Proverbs 1:20 NKJV). This phrase is not to be interpreted as an evil objective, but it rather asserts an intentional invitation to learn of her acumen or insight. The scripture also declares, "(She) *wisdom* has built her house, she has carved out her seven pillars" (Proverbs 9:1-6 NASB). These seven pillars are the representation of the seven spirits of God (Revelation 5:6). Wisdom is the representation of the first of the seven spirits which is before the throne of God. This is an

THE ASTUTENESS OF DIVINE WISDOM

incredible insight to recognize her as one of the attributes of God's spirit. We can note that Wisdom *"She"* stands before the throne of God in strength and might as in power.

The king Solomon associated wisdom with a feminine personality. He stated that, "Wisdom" had prepared a great banquet and set a table with bread and wine (Proverbs 9:5). Wisdom could also be equated to a hospitable persona and all believers can have a personal relationship with her by faith. This metaphor is linked to the psalm where David declared, "The Lord prepared a table before him." The construction of the Tabernacle that Moses made contained the table of shewbread within the holy Place (Hebrew 9:2). The Sages say that the bread is a representation of "the bread of His presence." The Bible declared that "God is the bread of life." Jewish history tells us that the shewbread that was placed in the tabernacle represented the twelve tribes of Israel. Therefore, the bread was replaced every week on their Sabbath, and their priest would eat the bread that was on display. This revealed that the divine presence of the bread of life was freshly provided and they could not depend on the same bread for all times.

The wine in scripture is likened to life. In the natural, wine is a beverage used that can cause intoxication, however, the metaphorical usage of wine here associates it to the presence of God and an essence of goodness. The Bible tells us that Jesus, on the night of the Passover, took the cup of wine and blessed it as a representation of His shed blood. The scripture stated that wisdom set bread and wine for the purpose of feasting or mingling. The spiritual reality of the bread comes down from Heaven and it intermingles with the wine. Therefore, the divine wisdom of God is likened to a recipe of the presence of God the Father, together with His Son and the Holy Spirit as they interact.

Jewish history states that there is a theoretical difference in the level of divine wisdom placed on the High priest and the Levites. The Lord calls those priests His servants and their assignment were to lead the nation into holiness and dedication. In the New Testament, Jesus Christ was identified as a priest as He walked in the excellence of wisdom. In one instance Jesus proclaimed that "He is the bread of Life." His analogy referred to spiritual and physical manna, He was literally likening the physical sustenance of food to the figurative means of spiritual food needed for their lives. The wisdom His disciples needed to be satisfied spiritually was to believe that He was the Messiah and there was a relationship with God the Father. Jesus continued to declare aloud, "If any man thirst, let him come to me, and drink. He that believeth on me, out of his belly shall flow rivers of living water" (John 7:37-38 KJV). The figurative speech referred to the word of God, and the water symbolizes life itself. Jesus is the word of God and His divine wisdom is the counsel of the spiritual pathway to life eternal.

The Proverbs states that wisdom is not reclusive, she gets involved in everyday life. The Bible says, "Wisdom is greatly creative, and she has the capacity to make godly decisions based on her knowledge, her strength is witty, and she has a shrewdness in her inventions" (Proverbs 8:12). These analogies are of the character of the Holy Spirit.

She *(wisdom)* sent forth her maidens, as she cries upon the highest places of the city. Her call is for the simple or humble and whosoever, to turn into her place of dwelling. Her plea is for those individuals who need understanding to come back or return to the Holy presence of God. She desires to provide love and insight to those that choose to be disobedient. The word of God tells us, *"The fear of the LORD is the beginning of wisdom and the knowledge of the Holy One there is understanding"* (Proverbs 9:10 NKJV).

King Solomon wrote that wisdom can be acquainted with the variance of ungodly wisdom. In the book of Ecclesiastes, he recognized that all the wealth, riches, and fame were all vanity without a relationship with the wisdom from God (Ecclesiastes 2-3). Wisdom was also identified as a female with an absurd character. The prophet Isaiah categorized ungodly wisdom as an attitude of a rebellious heart, towards the wisdom of God.

In the book of James, the apostle declared that there were two kinds of wisdom, and he admonished the people of Israel to act

THE ASTUTENESS OF DIVINE WISDOM

as brethren of the character of wisdom. *"Who among you is wise and understanding? Let him show by his good behavior his deeds in the gentleness of wisdom"* (James 3:13-18 NASB). Wisdom exudes light, His word is the light of the revelation of God. The bible mentions that the apostle Paul was not bound by the limitations of his human wisdom because of his encounter with the spirit of God. He conveyed spiritual wisdom through him to preach the gospel (1 Corinthians 2:13). In other words, Paul's words were not thought by human wisdom, he received revelation imparted by the Holy Spirit that was a combination of spiritual words and thoughts.

The Chronicles of Wisdom

The scripture chronicled the most characterization of wisdom in the book of Proverbs. When wisdom speaks, she accentuates the spiritual value she imparts to those who find her. Wisdom has presented true riches, honor, and an inheritance to the adulterous woman in Proverbs chapter seven. Wisdom highlights the fact that this adulterous woman in comparison to her wisdom is disgraceful and would lead men to poverty.

Here are feminine personifications of wisdom as it relates to the Holy Spirit as an attribute of God:

- Wisdom is a feminine persona of the spirit of God.
- Wisdom is foundational in the beginning of time and creation.
- Wisdom is the unseen; the invisible One, likened to the Holy Spirit.
- Wisdom exists in strength and unexplained power.
- Wisdom cries aloud; she has a voice of a trumpet.
- Wisdom pleas to men and all people.
- Wisdom comforts and nurtures (likened to a woman).
- Wisdom teaches and instructs in excellence, the

thing of revelation knowledge.
- Wisdom reproofs or brings correction like a mother does.
- Wisdom displays mercy and grace like the Holy Spirit does.
- Wisdom speaks truth, with honest integrity, falsehood is never intwined in her.
- Wisdom is divine and honorable, and there is no wickedness in her lips; mischief is not practiced in her personality.
- Wisdom speaks in righteousness and judgment, there is no immorality or injustice in her.
- Her words are not perverse or in presumption to her righteousness.
- Wisdom is greatly creative in interventions.
- She gives instruction, knowledge, and revelation that are more precious than gold or silver. She has worth.
- In her strength there is counsel and a diversity of revelation.
- She is strength to kings that reign, and princes that decree justice (Daniel 2:20-12).
- Wisdom loves! She loves even those that are unlovable.
- She loves those who seek her early or at a young age; for she reveals herself to them. She loves the life of those who chose to walk with the Lord God.
- Wisdom is wealthy; she possesses riches and honor (integrity).
- She possesses fruit better than gold and silver. In her are the fruits of the spirit of God (Galatians 5:22-23).
- She delights in the sons of men (humanity). She finds satisfaction in delight of men.
- Wisdom intercedes, testifies, and empowers.

THE ASTUTENESS OF DIVINE WISDOM

- Wisdom blesses us with life and favor of the Lord. Wisdom prolongs life with many years and brings peace (shalom) and prosperity (Proverbs 9:11).
- Wisdom hates evil men and prideful, arrogant people.
- Her justice is against those of a sinful soul. The judgment of those that hate wisdom is death.

"HAPPY is the man that findeth wisdom, and the man that getteth understanding. For the merchandise of it is better than the merchandise of silver, and the gain thereof than fine gold. She is more precious than rubies: and all the things thou canst desire are not to be compared unto her. Length of days is in her right hand, and in her left-hand riches and honor. Her ways are ways of pleasantness, and all her paths are peace. She is a tree of life, to them that lay hold of her: happy is everyone that retaineth her" (Proverbs 3:13-18 KJV).

The reference to this scripture is in the book of Genesis where it is read that there was a tree present in the Garden of Eden of Knowledge and Truth, *"the tree of life was also in the midst of the garden, and the tree of knowledge of good and evil"* (Genesis 2:9 KJV). This phrase indicates that there was a peculiar tree that has the personality of wisdom, and it proclaimed, *"For those who find me (wisdom), find life and receive favor from the LORD"* (Proverbs 8:35 NIV). The idiom expressed an invitation to the believer to seek the God of wisdom and to encourage their walk to be persistent. It offers life and sustenance of wisdom, and favor of God; that surpasses all-natural states to obtain the blessing of God.

King Solomon in his reference to wisdom and understanding had used the female character. He was in acknowledgement of the happiness and guidance that a woman could contribute to a man's life. His wise counsel equated wisdom, as a woman with the value of the beauty of precious stones. The king elaborated wisdom's charisma as of a peaceable woman whose possessions were of the tree of life and her attitude full of happiness, love, and the fear of the Lord, with all the gifts of the Spirit.

Wisdom is personified also with her relationship of her sisterly love. The Bible states that the kingdom of God is the foundation of wisdom and understanding. The Sages likened this relationship to a covenant marriage that causes an enhancement to oneness. They mentioned the impossibility to acquire wisdom without having understanding. They say that wisdom enriches understanding as wisdom is remarkably beautified in understanding to achieve their mission.

Hebrew scholars believe that the writing of the "Proverbs 31 woman" was written by Bathsheba to her son. She was the wife of King David and the mother of King Solomon, and the Sages say that Bathsheba had nicknamed Solomon as "Lemuel". The meaning of Solomon's name in Hebrew is "Man of Peace." This suggests that Solomon received wisdom and peace. According to a rabbi scholar, Solomon's nickname in Hebrew identified as "the King to whom God spoke" and another interpretation says, "The dedicated to God or devoted to God." In the book of Proverbs, his mother (Bathsheba) tried to caution Solomon on the prospective of a spiritual life as she warned him that there was a distinction to the life of a chosen king of Israel. In this case, Solomon was supposed to seek insight from God, and this required him to live a righteous and ethical life as a king. In the Proverbs Bathsheba spoke of a godly woman that was preferred to be her son's wife. Her attributes would pertain to a woman or wife that was proficient in the wisdom of God. However, in the scriptures, eventually Solomon ignored the spiritual aspect of his kingship. His character became marred by his attachment to ungodly women, and that lead him to unwise actions that were spiritual abominations to God.

Solomon's mother could be known as a wise woman. She understood the spiritual wisdom that was required to be successful as a king. As the wife to King David, she had firsthand knowledge of the failures and successes of her husband. Perhaps Bathsheba's life was overlooked in scripture, but her significance to Solomon was highlighted when she used her experiences to coach Solomon into becoming a wise son. Her situation was forced upon her and

THE ASTUTENESS OF DIVINE WISDOM

there was no mention of her faith in the God of Israel. The sins that she committed were mainly punishment and God's actions towards David caused her to endure all the sadness of their first-born son. Could it be through David's actions towards her husband Uriah also produced her humility and her desire for King Solomon was to influence him to become more penitent in his heart.

The Proverbs 31 Woman

The topic of a "Proverbs 31 woman" mainly gives the believer a description of what a woman of God should be like. However, the subject can also reflect the character of the righteous person who submits to the requirements concerning wisdom and understanding of God's commands.

The Sages suggest that it was Bathsheba's revelation of a wise or righteous woman. Even though there was not much revealed about Bathsheba's life before being one of David's wives, family lineage shows that she had some connection to an elite family. Her father, Eliam, was an elite vanguard of King David (2 Samuel 23:34) and her grandfather, Ahithophel, was a wise counselor to the king. Her insight may have caused her to question her situation against the righteousness and benefits of the spiritual wisdom of a woman.

Proverbs inquired: *"Who can find a virtuous woman? For her price is far above rubies. The heart of her husband doth safely trust in her, so that he shall have no need of spoil. She seeketh wool, and flax, and worketh willingly with her hands. She is like the merchants' ships; she bringseth her food from afar* (Proverbs 31:10-14 KJV). Traditionally, in the Jewish nation there were merchants, and the prophet Ezekiel explained that they did business in blue clothes, *"and broidered work in chests of rich apparel, bound with chords, and made of cedar, among thy merchandise"* (Ezekiel 27:24-25).

"She gets up while still night, she provides food for her family, and portions for her female servants. She considers a field and buys it out of her earnings, she plants a vineyard. She opens her arms to the poor and extends her hands to the needy. Her husband is respected at the city gate".

"She speaks with wisdom, and faithful instruction is on her tongue". She does not eat the bread of idleness. Her children arise and call her blessed; her husband also, and he praises her. Many women do noble things, but you surpass them all" (Proverbs 31:15-29 NIV).

The description of such a strong woman shows that her character is defined as a blessed one for "she is clothed with strength and dignity, she rises early to seek wisdom, and she concentrates her strength on building and generating wealth. She has no fear of her future, as she believes that wisdom is eternally faithful. When she speaks, her words are prudent and encouraging. She gives instructions with compassion and inspiration of God's wisdom from her obedience to the word of God" (Proverbs 31). Such a woman possesses virtue that is not bound with much of silver and gold. Such costly emeralds could not be compared to the origin of her wisdom; for her wisdom is only ordained from God our Father.

The bible tells us that in the last days, there will be an outpouring of the supernatural blessing of wisdom and revelation upon the men and women that desire a touch from God. Therefore, the Lord assured His people, *"It shall come to pass afterwards, that I will pour out my spirit upon all flesh"* and *"I will shew wonders in the heavens and in the earth, blood, and fire, and pillars of smoke"* (Joel 2:28, 30 KJV).

There is a fundamental truth of the blessings of God that is in the scriptures, *"When wisdom enters your heart, knowledge is pleasant to your soul"* (Proverbs 2:10 NKJV). Another verse declares, *"A wise man will hear and will increase learning"* (Proverbs 1:5 KJV). The reading and hearing of the word of God makes a tremendous impact on the standards of life, there is no searching of His understanding. Another scripture states that, the Lord gives power to the faint, and to them that have no might, He increases strength.

Chapter 7
The Astuteness of Divine Wisdom

"By Me kings reign and princes decree justice; by me, princes' rule."
(Proverbs 8:15-16 KJV)

The bible declares that *"The fear of the Lord is the beginning of wisdom; a good understanding have all those who do His commandments"* (Psalm 111:10 NKJV). The scripture also tells us, *"The fear of the Lord is the beginning of wisdom, and the knowledge of the Holy One is understanding. For by 'me' (Wisdom) your days will be multiplied, and the years of life will be added to you"* (Proverbs 9:10 NKJV). I remember hearing a Rabbi say that understanding the roots of Judaism is basically Christianity.

Wisdom proclaimed that, *"All the words of my mouth are in righteousness; there is nothing forward or perverse in them"* (Proverbs 8:8 KJV). This passage has given more insight on the authenticity of the spirit of God. *"I lead in the way of righteousness, in the midst of the paths of judgements: That I may cause those that love me to inherit substance; and I will fill their treasures"* (Proverbs 8:20-21 KJV). The word "lead" can be described as "a principal of uprightness or blamelessness." The "paths" can be referred to the way to honesty and impartiality in verdicts concerning the success of godly inheritance. In accordance to the persona of wisdom, there is no favoritism of persons and she is multilingual to speak in every tongue of every nation. Wisdom is customized to the spiritual perspective of the heart of a man. God, in His wisdom, created all men with an individual manifestation of knowledge of the Father.

The prophet Isaiah declares that the Messiah, Jesus Christ, is a fruit of Jesse (Jesse, David's father). In his comparison he likened our Messiah as the tree and a rod out of a stem, as the "branch" grown out of the roots. He portrayed that the blessing of the anointing upon Jesus was as the Spirit of God that literally rested upon him. Isaiah indicates that the anointing of God was inclusive of "the spirit of wisdom and understanding, the spirit of counsel and might, the spirit of knowledge, and the fear and revenge of the Lord."

In Jesus' days, the earth exploded to a ministry that operated in an authoritative factor of revelation of the blessings of wisdom. The Bible states that Jesus the Messiah did only what His Father inspired Him to do. On many occasions He did well and healed those that were sick and He delivered those that were oppressed of the devil. His sermons revealed the wisdom of God by the statement Matthew recorded when Jesus said, *"All things are delivered unto me of my Father: and no man knoweth the Son, but the Father; neither knoweth any man the Father, save the Son and he to whomsoever the son will reveal him"* (Matthew 11:29 KJV).

Wisdom is instrumental in the influence of winning souls for the kingdom of God. *"The fruit of righteousness is a tree of Life, and the one who is wise saves lives"* (Proverbs 11:30 NIV). In the book of Revelation, the spirit of wisdom revealed to John that He had undeniably seen all the works of man, not exempting the churches (Revelation 3:1). In the Proverbs wisdom declared, *"Counsel is mine, and sound wisdom: I am understanding, I have strength. By me kings' reign, and princes decree justice. By me Princes' rule, and nobles, even all the judges of the earth"* (Proverbs 8:14-16 KJV). In this phrase *"wisdom"* was personified as the power through which governance is proficient to function. King Solomon was a profound leader of his day (1 Kings 3:11-14). The apostle Paul stated that there was no authority except from God the Father (Romans 13:1).

Another proverb reveals that *wisdom* ensures wealth and prosperity in our life. It can be alleged that the fruit of wisdom is better than durable riches of fine gold and the choice between silver and rubies. Moreover, our righteousness and even all the things that may be desired cannot be equated to God's wisdom. The scripture declares *"It is the glory of God to conceal a matter, but the glory of kings is to search out a matter"* (Proverbs 25:2 NKJV).

THE ASTUTENESS OF DIVINE WISDOM

The Wisdom Gift of God

The apostle Paul tells us that the gift of God is given to men and women for the good of stimulating others (1 Corinthians 12:7). The gifts of God are not to be confused with the gift of the Spirit. The gift of wisdom, the word of knowledge, and the spirit of discernment are categories as knowing gifts. The gift of miracles, healing and faith are known as the power gifts. The gift of tongues, interpretation of tongues, and the gift of prophecy are all called speaking gifts. People are blessed with these gifts as the baptism of the Holy Spirit comes to light.

The Bible reveals that after the day of Pentecost experience (Acts 2:1-4), the disciples were filled with the Holy Spirit, and immediately, the believers began to walk in the spirit of God in wisdom and understanding. Paul mentions in his writings that they became known by their spiritual conversion and their walk. He highlighted that their blessings were the gift of the Spirit and the fruit of the Spirit. This gift of wisdom and knowledge are cohered to the gift of faith to produce healing, which also collaborated with faith and humility. He mentioned the gift of tongues that also interrelated to the gift of wisdom, knowledge, faith, love, joy, and peace in the Holy Ghost. It is God's desire to give all the blessings to those who walk in a measure of faith in Jesus Christ.

The fruits of the Holy Spirit are the attributes of God that a person possesses in a biblical term. The book of Galatians describes it as the spirit of love, joy, peace, patience, kindness, goodness, faithfulness, gentleness, and self-control (Galatians 5:22-23). The fruits of the Spirit in contrast display the development stages of the level of wisdom that causes the transformation of the character of a person to the image of God. This could be seen in natural gifts and talents as well as a person's demeanor, actions, words, and attitude.

Jesus addressed the function of the gift of the Spirit as merely the obedience to God commands. He told the people that if they walk in disobedience to God, they would be eternally separated from Him (Matthew 7:21-13). He pointed out that without the fruit of love, everything else is worthless. He said that the fruit of faith, love, and hope will always remain much longer than the gifts of prophecy, tongues, and the word of knowledge.

The influence of the Holy Spirit shapes our lives and living in that the leadership of the spirit of God is wisdom and understanding. Ephesians says that after you have accepted the Lord and believed in His word, you are marked with a seal by the Holy Spirit. *"For the gifts and calling of God are without repentance"* (Romans 11:29 KJV). Another translation says, *"The gifts and the calling of God are irrevocable"* (NKJV). God never changes His mind in respect to His promises. Once the Lord gives you a gift, He doesn't take it back. The gifts of God include the gift of His son Jesus Christ, and the gift of the Holy Spirit. The gifts of the Holy Spirit are: "Wisdom, Knowledge, Faith, Healing, Tongues, Love, Joy, Peace and Humility/Longsuffering." The blessings of God are given to whoever He chooses.

In the book of Revelation, the Menorah or Seven candlestand mentioned is a representative of the seven spirits of God (Revelation 1:12-13). It is a sacred emblem used in tabernacles as a representation of the Lord amidst the spirits of God. The menorah symbolizes the nation of Israel and their mission to bring light to the world (Isaiah 42:6). The middle candle stick is said to be taller than the other six sticks and the Sages say that it is the representation of the Counsel of the Lord. They say that the other six from left to right represent the fear of the Lord, the knowledge of God, the power of God, the understanding of God, the wisdom of God, and "Adonai's suffering" or Jesus Christ's suffering.

The stories behind the candles are the gifts of the Lord. John the revelator saw the candle sticks and the lights as the representation of the seven churches. It reveals that the Lord God is measuring the churches according to the light of His Counsel. The Bible tells us, "Your word is a lamp for my feet and a light on my path" (Psalms 119:105 NIV).

His gifts are limited to the churches, for the Lord reveals the state of the heart of the people in that day, and even today. John

THE ASTUTENESS OF DIVINE WISDOM

the revelator described the Lord as "the One with the seven spirits of God and the seven stars". As the Lord spoke to John, He relayed to him by his discernment, and the spirit of knowledge the message to the churches. *"I know your works, that you have a name that you are alive, but you are dead"* (Revelation 3:1 NKJV).

The Lord showed that the body of Christ was professing their belief towards God, but were not in a holy place or in purity with which the Lord could accept their declaration of faith. He saw their faith confession as superficial towards their love for Him. We must have a desire to receive the gifts of God, most importantly the gift of discernment and the gift of wisdom.

In the Hebrew Scripture there is one of the visions of Zachariah in comparison to the spirits of God. The Bible tells us that Zachariah saw a menorah or candle stand and the Lord spoke to him. He explained that Israel was brought out of Egypt and into Canaan by God's spirit, God's might, and His power. Zachariah received the revelation that all the gifts of God are obtained not by his own strength, nor by his power, but, by the spirit of God. *"Not by might, nor by power, but by my spirit"* (Zachariah 4:1-6 KJV).

A Hebrew Outlook on Wisdom

Hebraic scholars acknowledge that God is a spirit. He functions in the spirit of knowledge and wisdom. They explain that there are four progressions to the study of wisdom. On each level, the wisdom goes from elementary knowledge to a more advanced phase. Their outlook of divine wisdom is revealed in a biblical perspective and their analysis suggests that the topic is a great tool for measuring the actual phase of a person's wisdom. Their interpretation of wisdom is like a blessing and it is instrumental to the elevation of insight into the things of God. The scripture states that God called His children to reign on the earth as kings and priest (Revelation 5:10). They were mandated to increase in wisdom by studying and obeying the word of God.

UNDENIABLE WISDOM

A Jewish theologian states that, there are four levels of spiritual wisdom. The chore of scriptural interpretation or "exegesis" means "the critical explanation or interpretation of a text". According to the rabbinic theologians they illustrated the bases of wisdom as follows:

- First, in the scripture there is a simple meaning or an obvious standard of intelligence to the text of the biblical history.
- Secondly, in scripture there is a hint or figurative meaning beyond the simple or literal sense of the biblical text.
- Thirdly, there is an allegory of wisdom that causes the reader to inquire or search for the mysterious meanings of the text.
- Finally, there is a hidden mystery or the secret to understand that the meaning of the text is concealed.

The historical principle in the grammatical wisdom is classified in the four methods of the Jewish biblical exegesis abbreviated as "PaRDeS." This is an acronym of the following Hebrew words: "Peshat, Remez, Drash and Sod."

The first level *"Peshat"* is a Hebrew word for the searching out of a plain and simple (literal) meaning of the text. This level is the keystone of the literal sense of wisdom and understanding the scriptures. The scholars say that it is easy to neglect this level of wisdom, for it could cause a person to lose any real chance of an accurate understanding. For example, "who, where, and what happened" in the text is a literal sense. A simple illustration in context of the scriptures says, "Thou shall not steal." The reader should simply consider what this meant.

It is easy to use a pure imagination of the scriptures and the outcome will no longer derive the true meaning of the subject. Even Jesus used parables in His teaching to convey deeper meaning.

THE ASTUTENESS OF DIVINE WISDOM

"And he said unto them, He that has ears to hear, let him hear" (Mark 4:9-13 KJV). In this example, an explanation is to say that "anyone with ears should listen."

The Hebrew word for the second level is *"Remez."* This means *"to search out the hints"* or *"the depth."* There is an indication that there is something more to this text, which was intended to reinforce understanding. It implies that the text indirectly esteems the subject as an allegorical hint as vital to the presentation. For instance, the Bible tells us, Stephen knelt and cried with a loud voice. *"Lord, lay not this sin to their charge"* and he fell asleep (Acts 7:60 KJV). The hidden figurative speech that Steven uttered was beyond the literal sense. He merely pleaded with God for merciful judgment for those who stoned him before he died.

The third level is known in Hebrew as *"Drash"* and it includes moralistic parables. The text requires study or research for the comparative details. This level has hidden meanings and occurrences in the mysterious text. At this level of wisdom, both the hermeneutical and allegorical applications to the manuscript are required. The word *"hermeneutics"* means *"to have a portion of knowledge which is usually the specific interpretation applied to the text."* In the Bible, there are various levels of meanings and they tend to specify the focus on spiritual logic that is inclusive of the figurative wisdom, the moral wisdom, and an anagogical sense. The anagogical sense refers to the teaching of the scriptures that leads to eternal life and hope for the related future. However, the third level of wisdom is not pragmatic without the level one and two in the logical sense.

Jesus used "Drash" as he spoke in parables in his teachings. On one occasion Jesus told the Pharisees, *"For if you believed Moses, you would believe me; for he wrote about me. But, if you do not believe his writings, how will you believe my words?"* (John 5:46-47 NKJV). His statement was in the comparative language, and they needed to comprehend what He meant. Then, Jesus revealed to them that they never believed Moses, and therefore they couldn't recognize what He was affirming. The Bible tells us that God said to Moses,

UNDENIABLE WISDOM

"I will raise them up a Prophet from among their brethren, like unto thee, and I will put my words in His mouth; and he shall speak unto them all that I shall command him." (Deuteronomy 18:18 KJV). Jesus was again stating that He was the greater prophet that would come after Moses.

Finally, the level of wisdom known as *"Sod"* literally means, *"Secret."* The text consists of deeper revelation in which prophecies are exceptional. God's secrets or His fixed counsel are considered the hidden things that are not of this world. The "Sod" is the level whereby the mystery of God is concealed by His revelation. This supernatural insight is given by divine inspiration and revelation of the Lord God, to those that reverence His name. The level of Sod is a divine gift that consists of the mysterious treasures, and of spiritual and physical encounters. This fourth level unfortunately cannot function separately from the three other levels of wisdom, they are intertwined. An awesome illustration in the Bible declares, *"The secret of the Lord is with those who fear him; and He will show them His covenant"* (Psalm 25:14 NKJV). Ultimately, the Lord Jesus Christ was an exceptional model of the four levels the wisdom of God.

According to Moses, *"The secret things belong unto the Lord our God: but those things which are revealed belong unto us and to our children forever, that we may do all the words of this law"* (Deuteronomy 29:29 KJV). The Lord's involvement with Moses shaped the revelation to the prophets that they were chosen by God. The scriptures mention the prophet Samuel as one of the greatest prophets who walked in the Sod level of wisdom. There were several renowned prophets namely, David, Jeremiah, Joseph, Daniel, and even king Solomon that received the divine wisdom of God. Initially Solomon walked in such wisdom but in his old age he became torn between his wives and God.

Chapter 8
The Favor of God

*"For whoso findeth me (Wisdom) findeth life,
and shall obtain favor of the Lord."*
(Proverbs 8:35KJV)

The Bible tells us, *"Jesus grew in wisdom and stature, and in favor with God and man"* (Luke 2:52 NIV). *"For by grace you have been saved through faith, and that not of yourselves; it is a gift of God"* (Ephesians 2:8 NKJV). This scripture purposely states that the people who find wisdom shall obtain the favor of God. In other words, when a man or woman searches for the wisdom of God, they attain grace and wisdom as blessings from Him. Moreover, it is the favor of God that causes transformation of all things through wisdom. The definition of the word "favor" is described as "a demonstration of delight" in this context. *"For you bless the righteous person, Lord, surround him with favor as with a shield"* (Psalm 5:12 NASB).

God's favor is divine, and it is a power that comes from Heaven to cover our life to attract blessings towards us. This favor that comes from the Father in Heaven is demonstrated through mankind. The priestly blessing is consistent of the Favor of God. God permitted the priest to bless the people of God, it was their primary duty. The Bible says, "The Lord bless you and keep you" It was stated that when God blesses you with physically and spiritually it cannot fail or be taken away from you. The next verse says, "The Lord make His face shine upon you" (Numbers 6:25 NKJV). The Sages say that favor is in the eyes of God, of men and all that see us. "May God take away wrath from us and give us His peace, Shalom." Usually, the Hebrews bless their children and then all other family and associates to remove all the obstacles of sin. They say when the blessing is being spoken no one can pray at that moment but listen attentively and pray slowly and quietly.

UNDENIABLE WISDOM

According to the apostle Paul, *"God is able to make grace abound towards you"* (2 Corinthians 9:8 NKJV). The Psalmist proclaimed, "Let the favor of the Lord our God be upon us: and confirm for us the work of our hands; yes, confirm the work of our hands" (Psalm 90:17 NASB). His emphasis was customarily dependent upon God's favor as vital to his wisdom and success. The word of God declares that, "good men obtain favor from the Lord." In one commentary, it is mentioned that "favor is an act of kindness and it is preceded by goodwill as the preferential treatment shown to another person." It specified that an individual could find favor with God whenever they ceased from the struggle of their personal desires.

In the Hebrew language the word "favor" is *"chen."* The word for "favor" in Hebrew is associated with the words *"grace"* and *"mercy."* Chen is derived from the root word meaning pardon, favor, graciousness, compassion, and mercy. In a biblical perspective, the word "chen" denotes the merited favor of God towards a human being, or the favor of one toward another. Favor is extended with God's grace, and it is received in response to our prayer and righteous living. Therefore, the grace of God is comparable the favor of God. It can be said that grace is favor and blessings of God's kindness. In the book of Ephesians it declares, *"For it is by Grace you have been saved, through faith, and this is not from yourselves, it is the gift of God"* (Ephesians 2:8 NIV). This scripture can be translated as "God has given mankind the gift of salvation freely. "Salvation" is "Yeshua" and He was filled with wisdom and favor from God."

In the book of Psalm, David pleaded for the Lord to place His favor within his heart, and to give him grace according to His promise (Psalm 119:58). David recognized that the favor of God can only be experienced through the Lord. In other words, all other things such as blessings of the wisdom and knowledge of God will be revealed.

In the Bible, Noah found favor in the eyes of God (Genesis 6:8). *"God blessed Noah and his sons, and said unto them, be fruitful, and multiply, and replenish the earth"* (Genesis 9:1 KJV). Moses requested the favor of God as he pleaded for God to show him His glory and teach him His ways so that he may know God and continue to find favor with Him (Exodus 33:13). They were at Mount Sinai when they all experienced God's presence. Afterwards, Moses prayed for God to go with him and the people of Israel along their journey to the promise land. The Sages say, when Moses asked God for His glory, the Lord revealed to Moses His character of a gracious personality (Exodus 34:6). The Psalmist had the revelation of Moses, and proclaimed, *"The Lord is merciful and gracious, slow to anger, abounding in mercy"* (Psalm 103:8 NKJV).

In all the encounters Moses experienced from the burning bush to Mount Sinai, he received revelation of the wisdom of God, and these resulted in Moses' performance of miracles. The scriptures tell of Daniel the prophet and Mary the mother of Jesus Christ was highly favored by God. There was an angel of God who conveyed their messages from God. The angel sent to Daniel declared, *"O man greatly beloved, fear not"* (Daniel 10:19 KJV). Likewise, he said to Mary, *"Hail, thou that art highly favored, the Lord is with thee: blessed are thou among women!"* (Luke 1:28 KJV).

The favor of God is instrumental in the righteous walk of the believer. The Psalmist proclaimed, *"The steps of a good man are ordered by the Lord"* (Psalm 37:23 KJV). One of my favorite verses of scripture says, *"Trust in the Lord with all your heart, and lean not on your own understanding. In all your ways acknowledge Him, and He shall direct your paths"* (Psalm 3:5-6 NKJV). The path that is referred to here is the righteous way that leads to the levels of wisdom and discernment. The apostle Matthew declared, *"But seek first the kingdom of God, and all these things shall be added to you"* (Matthew 6:33 NKJV).

In one of the stories of Israel's oppression, there was the king Jehoahaz that reigned. The scenario was a judgement from God for the sins of Israel, but King Jehoahaz prayed, and the Lord granted Israel favor over the King of Syria. The King Jehoahaz sought the favor of the Lord as he had seen the oppression of Israel and how the king of Syria oppressed them, and the Lord listened to him (2

Kings 13:4). The king's repentance and prayers to God granted God's favor. Isaiah prophesied that Israel would overcome their enemies. Isaiah stated that God approved of some of the people of Israel because of their heart condition and He favored them for their obedience towards Him. *"These are the ones I look on with favor: those who are humble and contrite in spirit, and who tremble at my word"* (Isaiah 66:2 NIV).

The gift of favor is a privilege to every believer just as the gift of wisdom from a spiritual aspect. According to the apostle Paul, as believers, we are all blessed with spiritual gifts from God. *"For to one is given by the Spirit the word of wisdom; to another the word of knowledge by the same Spirit"* (1 Corinthians 12:8 KJV). These gifts are unique, and in the plan of salvation there is a measure of favor and grace. The apostle Peter stated that God predestined the death of Jesus Christ to save the world from their sins (1 Peter 1:20).

In this subject, I believe that every individual was born with a measure of grace as a gift of favor from God. He also proclaimed the plan of salvation from the spiritual aspect is the gift of the wisdom of God. *"Before the foundation of the world God chose Jesus Christ. God's plan determined that He would die for the sins of the world"* (1 Peter 1:20).

Wisdom Proclaims Love!

Apostle Paul assured us that "wisdom" was revealed through the foretelling messages of God's prophets. The scriptures associate wisdom with a personality who proclaims that there are benefits to having a relationship with her. Wisdom declares, *"I love them that love me; and those that seek me early shall find me"* (Proverbs 8:17 KJV). Wisdom declares to those who would love her that she conveys honor, riches, life, and the favor of God. She always measures your love by the amount you attend to her.

The psalmist declared, *"O God, you are my God; early will I seek you; my soul thirst for you; my flesh longs for you in a dry and thirsty land where there is no water. I have looked for you in the sanctuary, to see your power and your glory. Because your lovingkindness is better than life, my lips shall praise you"* (Psalms 63:1-6 NKJV).

Wisdom desires for you to seek her early in the morning. The Psalmist proclaimed, *"In the morning, Lord, you will hear my voice; in the morning, I will present my prayer to you be on the watch"* (Psalm 5:3 NASB). The Bible tells us that Jesus prayed early in the morning, and he prayed at night as well. Jesus, after prayer, had significant events that occurred throughout His life. In other words, Jesus sought out wisdom early in the mornings and the favor of God was manifested throughout the day.

According to the Bible, *"Wisdom called out to all men, and understanding raised her voice. She called in the highest point along the way, she cries out by the gates, at the entry of the city, and at the entrance of the doors. She cries the loudest of a persevering voice that warns of danger to her friends."* The interpretation of her calling is to all mankind, she stands where the business transactions would transpire and at the entrances where people would go in and out of the city. The Bible confirms that "wisdom stands where paths meet" (Proverbs 8:2).

The favor of God is love simplified through wisdom. The logical characteristics of wisdom are comprised of natural and spiritual definitions towards humanity. The spiritual wisdom helps the natural aspect to flourish physically.

Here are some outcomes to analyze:

- Wisdom helps you to do the right things.
- Wisdom conveys the right people for your friendships.
- Wisdom teaches us to be a good husband, a good wife, a good mother, a good father, and to be good children.
- Wisdom leads you to the right partner for marriage.
- Wisdom gives you direction for the divine helpers and the right contacts to do investments.
- The Wisdom of God gives us an understanding

- of the "Times and Seasons" of the Lord, for the appointed time for offerings and more reasons to praise and rejoice the Lord.
- There are many great verses of spiritual wisdom in the bible that are usually illuminating to the perspective of a blessed life. The apostle Peter talks about the relationship with wisdom (2 Peter 1:3-13).

According to His divine power, He has given us all things we need for godly life through our knowledge; that pertain to life and godliness or wisdom.

- Wisdom will be the multiplication of grace and peace.
- Wisdom is knowledge that will increase through faith.
- The believer will have divine power and divine nature.
- They will walk in an unusual life and His godliness
- They will have Hidden glory (insight) and virtue.
- They will walk in His exceeding, supernatural grace, and precious promises.
- They will manifest fruitfulness and prosperity.
- They will be election sure and everlasting life.
- Wisdom dispels darkness from our lives.
- Wisdom rewards those who trust in God.

Wisdom is overt and can be produced by implementing these principles in our everyday life. According to the prophet Hosea, true wisdom is correlated with trusting in God.

"Blessed is the man that trust in the Lord, and whose hope is in the God. For he shall be like as a tree planted by the waters, which spreads out its roots by the river, and will not see fear when heat comes; but its

THE FAVOR OF GOD

leaf will be green; and will not be anxious in the year of drought, nor will cease from yielding fruit" (Jeremiah 17:7-8 NKJV).

The apostle Paul declares that there is a wisdom that is divine, this wisdom can only be given by the Holy Spirit at work in you (1 Corinthians 2:14). This divine wisdom is given to those who desire to know the Lord Jesus Christ. In fact, God gives spiritual wisdom to us when we ask Him for it. The apostle James tells us that we are required to be in dialogue with God it is beneficial to the gift of God in spiritual wisdom. The Bible says that as the church prayed and fasted, the Holy Ghost said to separate Barnabas and Saul for the work of the Lord (Acts 13:1-3). The gift of wisdom is the distributer of the individual perception by the spirit of the Lord.

A scripture in Proverbs declares, *"Blessed is the man who listens to me, watching daily at my gates, waiting at the posts of my doors." For whoever finds me finds life and obtain favor from the Lord. But who sin against me wrongs his own soul; all those who hate me love death"* (Proverbs 8:34 NKJV). This scripture emphasizes that listening is a crucial key to wisdom. God commanded the people to watch, wait, and search for Him. These three action words are the technique of a daily restoration of His wisdom. These teachable moments are required to watch or seek God for the opportune moments of learning from Him.

Amos the prophet reiterated, those who seek Him shall live (Amos 5:4). The phrase "to seek God" stands to express a consultation from God and by His prophets even on a purely nonspiritual matter. Amos was teaching the fundamental principle that to find God you must seek Him. Amos proclaimed to Israel and all men, that it is the practical way of life. This meant that God can only be sought in the way He desires to give His revelation, which is through worship and prayer. The psalmist David declared that God is the fountain of life, those in His light shall see light. This phrase can be interpreted as light being the true meaning of wisdom and knowledge.

The Sages say that in the past, when a king or person wanted to inquire of God, they would go the prophet and he would seek the Lord on their behalf. These prophets were known as seers in those times and they were noted to have a spiritual eye to perceive and interpret eternal truth. The word, "Seer," initially meant "the one to whom divine revelations are made." It was Jewish custom to inquire of the Lord by their prophets. The Bible tells us the story of Rebekah, who inquired of the Lord for counsel concerning her pregnancy (Genesis 25:22). She personally received a response from the Lord, and He revealed that there were twins within her womb. They would form two great nations; she named her sons Jacob and Esau. The scripture says that Moses became a prophet and he inquired of the Lord on behalf of the people of Israel.

The king David in his writings, made a distinction in the passage about the blessed man, David proclaimed that:

> *"Blessed is the man who walks not in the counsel of the ungodly, nor stands in the path of sinners, nor sitteth in the seat of the scornful: but his delight is in the law of the Lord. and in His law he meditates day and night. He shall be like a tree planted by the rivers of water, that brings forth fruit in its season, who's leaf also, shall not wither; and whatever he does shall prosper"*
> (Psalms 1:1-3 NKJV).

The idiom of the blessed one refers to the blessings bestowed upon someone as of a gift from God. David gave a clear explanation of the identity of the righteous man. He established that wisdom divided the humans into two categories. In David's wisdom, he revealed that his concern was for the wealth and purpose of the peoples' destiny. He pointed out that there was not a third category to contemplate. Moreover, his son Solomon penned his confession, and declared his desire for the wisdom of God. He stated, *"A man's heart plans his way, but the Lord directs his steps"* (Proverbs 16:19 NKJV). King Solomon recognized that it is better to be humble in the spirit of the simple, than to be separated with the rewards of the proud or arrogant.

THE FAVOR OF GOD

In the book of John, Jesus declared, *"He who feeds on me will live because of me"* (John 6:57 NKJV). He is the truth and the life to everyone who accepts Him as their Lord and Savior. A profound comment from a Minister once caught my attention, his remark was, "God doesn't need us, but we need God!" It was the thought of how I do need God and He endows His wisdom and discernment within me. Moreover, God causes the blessing of Abraham to enrich our lives as we draw closer in an intimate relationship with Him. God's love is the abundance of wisdom and the continual knowledge which establishes boundaries in our lives. These guidelines of the spirit of God introduce godly gifts that include the gift of salvation, and the gift of purification from God.

Chapter 9
Wisdom is Transferable

"The secret things belong to the Lord our God, but those things which are revealed belong to us and to our children forever."
(Deuteronomy 29:29 NKJV)

In the scriptures, we read that the foundation of wisdom is supernatural. Only God revealed the unexplained source of wisdom and yet today we still have unresolved question pertaining to the gift of wisdom. In many instances, wisdom is transferrable through the Holy Spirit, for true wisdom is the Holy Spirit. I have recognized that the Holy Spirit would rest on a person and live within their heart, or actually would lift off a person, in other words depart. The Bible tells us that King Saul walked for a period in disobedience, and the spirit of God lifted. As a result, there was no tangible communication between him and God.

The scripture reveals that the spirit of God rested upon Jesus Christ (Yeshua). This specifies that God lived within His heart. The prophet Isaiah foretold that the spirit of the Lord will rest upon Him (Messiah); the spirit of wisdom and understanding, the spirit of counsel and strength, the spirit of knowledge and the fear of the Lord (Isaiah 11:2). The apostle John stated that Jesus breathed on the disciples to receive the Holy Spirit (John 20:22). This was a transfer of anointing. Evidently, Matthew gave the episode of Jesus transferring authority and to drive out impure spirits and to heal sickness and diseases (Matthew 10:1 NIV). The only way for them to operate in such power is with divine wisdom.

In the book of Exodus, God spoke to Moses and asked him to bring the 70 Elders to the mount so that God could impart His wisdom to them (Exodus 24:1). The Sages said that the chiefs were mostly of the distinct group amongst the Israelite tribes, and they began to serve the people with knowledge as judges for all times.

His glory is transferrable, and these 70 Elders received an infilling of His presence long before the book of Acts. The amazing part of the story is the two of the elders that were still in their tents as the other sixty-eight went to the mountain to meet with God. Joshua went to Moses objecting that the two elders should be stopped, for as they remained in the camp, they were heard prophesying as the glory of God fell upon them. Their names were recorded as Eldad and Medad, they too were filled with the holy presence. It reveals that God's presence was not limited to a certain location or people. Interestingly, their names are meaningful in the Hebrew language. The name "Eldad" in Hebrew means "God has loved," and the name "Medad" means "Love of God" or "Favored of God" (Numbers 11:16-25).

There was the transference at the end of Moses' days, when God instructed Moses concerning Joshua, the son of Nun, that he should place his hand upon Joshua to anoint his head with oil. As a young man Joshua experienced the same seasons of the wilderness with Moses and this was beneficial to him. He understood that the wisdom of God was upon Moses. He was present at Mount Sinai when Moses received many instructions concerning Israel's welfare. Joshua and the people knew their obedience to Moses' authority was critical to their victory. Therefore, when Joshua was anointed by God, he was imparted with the same blessings to mature and flourish with great authority, to overcome and fulfill the task of journeying to the Promise land. The Bible says, *"Now Joshua the Son of Nun was full of the spirit of wisdom, for Moses had laid his hands on him; so, the children of Israel listened to him and did as the Lord had commanded Moses"* (Deuteronomy 34:9 NKJV).

Israel's Exodus was not just a ticket to escape the bondage of the Egyptians. God chose the Hebrew people for Himself, to be a nation of priests and kings. The Lord desired to have a special relationship with them so that He could impart wisdom in His people. Their journey to Mount Sinai was preparation for the encounter with His glory. The Sages say that they experienced an impartation of wisdom and understanding. God equipped the

WISDOM IS TRANSFERABLE

Israelites to keep and obey all the statues and commands, or in other words the "dos and don'ts" for a successful life. According to the Scholars, at birth everyone has an amount of wisdom that is divinely imparted. However, their assignment has limitations without the holy presence of God. The scripture tells us that at Mount Sinai, the atmosphere was filled with the glorious presence of God and His manifestation from above initiated an infilling of wisdom upon the people. The writer of Exodus articulated that the people became full of wisdom. Moses confirmed that God's presence propelled the people into wisdom and knowledge, to obey the word of God. Moreover, they all received insight to build and design the tabernacle for God.

Moses recounted, in the book of Deuteronomy, a brief history of the Jewish experiences in Egypt and in the wilderness at Mount Sinai. The people were baptized in God's presence which foreshadowed His Holy Spirit in the book of Acts 2. Moses concluded that their encounter was of significance to God and His interaction was to accentuate their relationship forever. As Moses proclaimed, *"The secret things belong to the Lord God, but those things which are revealed belong to us and to our children"* (Deuteronomy 29:29 NIV).

At Sinai, the Holy Spirit was present as they experienced the wisdom of God in a transferrable manner. There was a testimony of a man known as *Bezalel*, the son of Uri, of the tribe of Judah, who God endowed with the spirit of wisdom. Moses declared that Bezalel was filled with the spirit of God, in wisdom and understanding, in the knowledge and in all manner of workmanship. Moses mentioned that it was the spirit of God within Bezalel that caused him to design artistic works, he received wisdom to work in gold, silver, and bronze. The Lord anointed him to be skilled in cutting jewels for setting, in carving wood, and to work in all manner of artistic workmanship (Exodus 35:30-35). Bezalel's contribution to the building of the tabernacle of God was worthy of admiration.

Jewish history says that Bezalel was the husband of Moses' sister Miriam. He was from the lineage of David for he was the son of Ori and the grandson of Hur. Some Sages state that he was a young man, when he received the baptism of the spirit of wisdom and knowledge. This supports the notion that all skillful gifts of wisdom come from the Father in Heaven and this is enlightening. One Hebrew scholar says that Bezalel was likened to Noah and his prime purpose was to build a dwelling place for God. He made a comparison of Bezalel to the Messiah, from the Hebrew meaning of his name. The Hebrew name "Bezalel" has the divine meaning of "in the shadow or protection of God". The Sages say that Bezalel was on Mount Sinai under the shadow of God and there he received his vision to build the tabernacle for God (Exodus 31:1-6).

There was mention in the Bible, of another righteous man named *Aholiah*. The Bible tells us that God put His wisdom inside Bezalel's heart for him to have the ability to teach Oholiah, the son of Ahisamach, of the tribe of Dan. His assistant carpenter *"Oholiah" or "Aholiah"* name in the Hebrew is known as *"my father's tent,"* which refers to the tabernacle. Amazingly, his father's name *"Ahisamach"* means *"brother of help"* or *"helpful"* in Hebrew. In this period, the wisdom of God was transferred through his teaching of knowledge and understanding. The Sages state that Betzelel's assistant Aholiad was skillful in the invention of engraving and embroidery. He was responsible for the design and creativity of the tabernacle curtains and he was also involved in the fashioning of the Ark of the Covenant (Exodus 31:6).

There were others present who received the spiritual anointing in the essence of engraving, designing, and tapestry making in the colors of blue, purple, and scarlet as well as threads and fine linen. You can read of the design and creativity of the tabernacle, the vessel, and their dimensions in the book of Exodus, Chapter 35.

We read of the women who received diverse wisdom as well, and they spun the yarn for the fine linen fabric with their hands. There were other Israelite males that received wisdom to engrave and embroider the garments for the tabernacle of God. As God instructed Moses, the ones that He endowed with the spirit of wisdom within them made the garments for the high priest, Aaron.

WISDOM IS TRANSFERABLE

It was to be a consecrated outfit which would be for the particular purpose of the Holy place. There were special garments designed for the priests to wear when they were ministering in the tabernacle (Exodus 28:3). Aaron was anointed with the spirit of wisdom as the high priest to minister to God in the Holy of Holies to consecrate the children of Israel.

The philosophy of wisdom is to obey and meditate on God's laws. The word "philosophy" means "to have the ability to think or act utilizing knowledge, an experience, understanding, common sense, and insight". Joshua was commanded by Moses to have the philosophy of wisdom. According to Moses he was to obey the book of the Laws and to meditate on them day and night (Joshua 1:8 KJV). The key here is that Joshua was to respect all that the Lord required of him and to utilize his knowledge and experiences in the ways of God to continue the task which was before him. The benefit of Joshua's persistent choice of wisdom would result with the blessing of much insight, good health, and possessions (wealth). I submit that a believer desiring God's wisdom should experience the favorable outcome of walking in health and prosperity.

The Word of Knowledge

In the book of Exodus, God revealed to Moses in the burning fire that "He is the God of the living, and not the dead." The Sages say that Moses had a glimpse of the past and future of Israel and he understood that the patriarchs were in Heaven. In the New Testament, Jesus reveals himself, saying, *"I am the God of Abraham, the God of Isaac, and the God of Jacob"* (Luke 20:38 NIV). Jesus asserted that He existed before Abraham, Isaac, and Jacob. The Bible teaches us that God and the Holy Spirit existed before the universe, for He is beyond the physical laws that govern the world (Psalm 90:2). Furthermore, "Yeshua is the same yesterday, today and forever."

Jesus emphasized that it was essential for Him to live by the word of God, in other words, the spirit of wisdom. Jesus quoted

Moses and declared, *"It is written: Man shall not live on bread alone, but on every word that comes from the mouth of God"* (Matthew 4:4 NIV). The natural mouth is referred to as a doorway or gateway that allows entry to things. The Hebrew word for mouth is *"peh"* and can be sometimes translated as "the command." Another insight says that the Mouth of God in Hebrew is the word "Megilla" which symbolizes the word for "Stroll" or "Volume." It can be referred to as the original source of intake of life's sustenance and revelation knowledge that comes from God. The prophet Moses declared, *"He humbled you and let you go hungry, and He fed you with manna which you did not know, nor did your fathers know, in order to make you understand that man shall not live on bread alone, but man shall live on everything that comes out of the mouth of God"* (Deuteronomy 8:3 NASB). The psalmist David revealed, *"The entrance of your words give light; it gives understanding to the simple"* (Psalm 119:130 NKJV). This phrase shows that the word of God brings insight and revelation to the humble to receive spiritual gratification to clear all our perception. The word of God can be likened to spiritual food to the humble soul that walks with the Lord God and obeys His laws. (It can self-restraint everyone from all sins and evil actions).

Spiritual wisdom is correlated to the "word of knowledge" or "the utterances of knowledge." The Bible tells us that God operates in His Wisdom through the person of the Holy Spirit and the Spirit gives the believer the ability to prophesy. The spirit of wisdom consists of revelation and spiritual discernment into present and future events. The apostle Paul clarified that the spiritual gift from God is for righteous living (1 Corinthians 12:8) and he admonished all believers to desire spiritual gifts from God. The men and woman who are blessed with the spirit of wisdom and knowledge are beneficial to all mankind. In his writings, he stated that wisdom of God is for the edification of the saints, the church, and the nations. The Lord administers levels of spiritual growth and discernment through the spirit of wisdom and the Holy Spirit enables the believer to effectively fulfil their divine destiny.

WISDOM IS TRANSFERABLE

Traditionally, in the Jewish culture the prophet of God was called a Seer. The Hebrew meaning of the word "seer" is "man of God". They were the chosen ones who feared God and had insight and discernment. They exercised wisdom to give incisive counsel or worthy instructions to kings and their nations. The prophet Samuel was called a seer, and, in his days, the Israelite people were guided in the things of God through a moral mouthpiece of the Lord. Samuel and other prophets were chosen to speak on behalf of God because the Holy Spirit had not yet come. In many instances, Samuel distinctly operated by the spirit of wisdom and knowledge.

The Bible tells us that the Lord spoke to Samuel and revealed who was the one He wanted him to anoint as king over Israel. The scenario of Saul and his father's donkeys created the opportunity for the prophet Samuel to discern the man God had chosen to be the first king over Israel. As Samuel entered at the city gate and they encountered each other, the spirit of wisdom and knowledge showed Samuel that this was the man. Saul received the prophecy that all was well with his father's donkeys, but his purpose was to be fulfilled. The conversation between Saul and Samuel made an impact on Saul, then Samuel insisted that they meet the following day so he could reveal what was within his heart (1 Samuel 9:15-20). In this revelation Samuel revealed many secret things to Saul through the help of the spirit of God. The next story tells us that it was God who had to reveal to the prophet Samuel the son of Jesse, who looked insignificant but was God's choice for the next king of Israel (1 Samuel 16:1). This shows that Samuel would have chosen the wrong son without the spirit of wisdom of God.

Jewish scholars refer to the captivity of the Israelites as part of the period that the Hebrew boys sought the wisdom of God. The Bible noted that they were among the wise men in Babylon and the Hebrew boys were exceptional. The four children mentioned were educated in skills of all learning and wisdom; there was one called Daniel that had excellence in understanding in all visions and dreams (Daniel 1:17).

One day the wise men in Babylon were called to interpret the pharaoh's dream and the scripture says that they all failed to discern his dreams, hence, a sentence of execution was decreed for all those that were deemed wise in intuition. Daniel became aware of the situation and their demise; he took courage to approach the pharaoh and request time be given to him for an answer to the dream. The Pharaoh permitted Daniel a few days as he explained that it took time to seek God. Daniel operated in profound wisdom and he gathered his brethren to fast and pray to ask God for help. The key point here is that Daniel called upon the God of their fathers, Abraham, Isaac, and Jacob. As he was praying for a period, the spirit of wisdom revealed the understanding of Pharaoh's dream (Daniel 2:47). Afterwards, Daniel was equipped to convey the interpretation of the dream to the Pharaoh. The spiritual wisdom is shown in Daniel's prayer of acknowledgment to God: "*Blessed be the name of God forever and ever, for wisdom and might are His. And He changes the times and the seasons; He removes kings and sets up kings; He gives wisdom to the wise and knowledge to those who have understanding*" (Daniel 2:20-21 NKJV).

In the book of Genesis, there was another scenario of the pharaoh in Egypt who desired an interpretation of his dreams. Joseph, the son of Jacob, was a captive in the land and he interpreted the Pharaoh's dreams. His spiritual intelligence-initiated praise and acknowledgement from the pharaoh that Joseph's God had made him unusual for he told the pharaoh his dreams, then he interpreted the dreams. Joseph functioned in the spirit of wisdom and knowledge, and the divine inspiration initiated the pharaoh to release Joseph from the prison, and to elevate him to the position of Governor of Egypt. The spirit of God was with Joseph and the restoration of his experience was a manifestation of God's wisdom in his circumstances. The prophet Joel declares that the Lord promises to restore all our years of youthfulness and the possessions of loss.

We read that the prophet Elisha had a reputation of operating in spirit of wisdom. His utterances displayed his ability to discern

WISDOM IS TRANSFERABLE

the manifestation of the spirit of God. In the history of the Jewish writings, Elisha was said to have given counsel to kings for the affairs of Israel. At one juncture, the Israelites were facing the catastrophe of war against the Syrian king. Elisha gave the king of Israel the details of the traps that his enemy had plotted beforehand. The Bible says that Elisha's wisdom caused the Israelites' army to be preserved from destruction and they were victorious in their battles (2 Kings 6:8-12). The Bible mentions that the prophet Elisha doing this repeatedly. Another account states that the king of Syria became troubled after many defeats and he began to inquire of his servant if there were any traitors found amongst his army. Then, one of his servants spoke up and declared to the king that it was a seer in Israel called Elisha who revealed the king's plot that was uttered in his bed chamber to the king of Israel. The news caused the king to be terribly angry and he began a conspiracy to take off the head of Elisha, the prophet.

In the Book of Kings, it tells of a prayer meeting happening at the home of Elisha where the Elders had congregated. They were seeking God and the prophet received a word of knowledge from the Lord (1 Kings 21:21). Immediately, Elisha disclosed the revelation, and they were prepared for what was about to transpire. He stated that there was a messenger on his way to his house and he was sent by the wicked king of Syria. In the same revelation, Elisha received a vision that the king himself was approaching behind his messenger. Elisha made plans to avert the situation so that there would be no causalities. He suggested that they restrain the messenger within the closed door when he arrived and then open the door to the king and avoid his command to the servant to be executed. In this scenario Elisha's wisdom caused lives to be saved again in Israel. Elisha's spiritual discernment provided the necessary instructions so that the elders could affect the king of Syria and his messenger.

This fascinating story revealed a vital function of the spirit of God logically and spiritually. The prophet Elisha, as their spiritual leader, was aware of God's spirit to protected God's people from the enemy. The spirit of wisdom is much need in the body of Christ today.

The spirit of wisdom is demonstrated of the divine wisdom in Peter and John as they were entering by the door of the synagogue. The Bible tells us that Peter fastened his eyes upon the lame man. The word "fastened" could also be explained as "an intense stare." The lame man would have been familiar with Peter and John going to the synagogue. As apostles of Jesus Christ, he greeted them with an expectancy of receiving something in the form of money. Peter perceived that the lame man was eager to accept his teaching and he immediately offered him the healing power of Jesus Christ. As, Peter declared, *"Silver and gold I have none; but such as I have give I thee: in the name of Jesus Christ of Nazareth, rise up and walk"* (Acts 3:6 KJV). The scripture tells us that immediately, Peter took him by the right hand and lifted him up. Instantaneously, the lame man received strength and rose on his feet, leaping and walking (Acts 3: 6-9). I submit that the spirit of wisdom can break every yoke of bondage in our lives in Jesus Name.

The perfect example of the divine gift of wisdom and discernment is Jesus Christ. His ministry showed the coherence of the gift of wisdom and knowledge. The Bible says that even as a young boy, Jesus grew and became strong in the spirit and filled with wisdom (Luke 2:40). In an earlier chapter, His wisdom was discussed, however, they pointed out that Jesus was twelve when he began display theological knowledge of the word of God in the synagogue. There was mention of Jesus being found in the company of the doctors of doctrines or "Sages" and they were greatly amazed at the wisdom of His answers.

The apostle John described that Jesus walked in the wisdom and revelation of God. When Jesus called Philip to follow Him, Phillip at once brought his brother Nathanael to see the Messiah of Israel. The fact that Jesus approached Nathanael instantly and called his name made Nathanael retort with a question. Nathanael became curious about how Jesus would have known his name. In Jewish culture, a child's name is very important. The name *Nathanael* in Hebrew means, "God has given" or "Gift of God". Then, Jesus

WISDOM IS TRANSFERABLE

replied cordially to Nathanael, *"Before Philip called you, when you were under the fig tree, I saw you"* (John 1:47-50 NKJV).

The Bible says that Nathanael immediately acknowledged Jesus as "Rabbi". He understood the spiritual aspect of the word of God and this began Nathanael's ministry. I often wonder if there was something Jesus revealed to Nathanael, concerning what he was doing under the fig tree. Maybe, Nathanael was praying to God for a deliverer at that moment. John never mentioned what Nathanael was doing; however, it seemed extremely significant for Nathanael to react with such an instantaneous conversion to Jesus' word of knowledge.

There is a great need for the gift of wisdom and knowledge today. Many believers lack such knowledge, and it is necessary for the believer to have a perceptive heart towards the mysteries of God. Even the church has a deficiency to these teachings which would guide God's people into the realm of their relational desires. The clarification of how to seek the wisdom of God is throughout the reading of the word of God. There should be a desire for the Holy Spirit to teach and reveal the gifts of God which are beneficial to every born-again believer as inheritance. In one of His teachings, Jesus said to His disciples, *"When he, the Spirit of truth, is come, he will guide you into all truth: for he shall not speak of himself; but whatsoever he shall hear, that shall he speak: and he will show you things to come"* (John 16:13 KJV).

The only way, as a believer, to operate in such miracle working power is to allow the Holy Spirit to work within our hearts. Here I would keep it simple to say that these supernatural workings are all relatively connected with truth, for there are gifts of healing, deliverance, salvation, discernment, and the word of knowledge. The apostle Mark made the statement that Jesus ordained the twelve disciples to be part of His ministry and to send them forth to teach and preach, and to be empowered to heal sicknesses, and to cast out devils (Mark 3:14-15). The book of Matthew states that *"He gave them the power"* (Matthew 10:1).

It is unwise not to be knowledgeable of the strategies the serpent, that Old Devil, as Jesus called him. The Bible tells us not to be ignorant of his schemes or to be caught by surprise.

Chapter 10
The Curiosity of Job

"Who has put wisdom in the mind?"
(Jobs 38:36 NKJV)

There is a story of a man called Job in the Bible whose dilemmas surrounding his life, and his tragedy resulted in devastation to his entire family. Job's situation initiated the demand for answers and at this juncture he sought counsel. The Bible says that these wise men (counsel) had contributed to their society in ways of accrued experiences and observations of life events from former generations of natural, civil, and religious affairs (Job 12:12). They were perhaps the wise men that understood the word of God and give counsel pertaining to such knowledge. However, their wisdom did not exceed the counsel of the "Ancient of Days".

The Sages state that wisdom comes with age. However, in the case of Job's friends, their initial thought was of a natural wisdom, and they alleged that Job had done a terrible sin against God. Their questions show that they were clueless as to why Job had experienced such loss. The Bible by no means mentioned that his friends prayed and sought counsel from the Lord concerning Job's situation. Just a side note here: on the other hand, Daniel sought the Lord in prayer. Their lack of wisdom in this scenario caused them to trigger more discouragement to Job, and their lack of counsel initiated the many appropriate questions that Job concealed within his heart.

This revelation shows that Job began to intertwine his inquisitive traits to the capacity of the wisdom of man. Job directed his questions to God, the creator, *"who put wisdom in the inward parts of a man"* (Job 38:36). The scripture was not explicit of the reason why Job's interest was fixed on nature and wisdom, but Job's diversity of thoughts had many surfaces for there were accumulated demands.

In Job's quest, the understanding of wisdom and its origin was enlightening. I believe in this story it reveals the limitation of the knowledge man possesses concerning the things of God. The second question Job asked the Lord was of the whereabouts of wisdom, *"Where can wisdom be found?"* and *"Where does understanding dwell?"* (Job 28:12 NIV). Job could not fathom how the proficiency of wisdom is positioned within the human's heart and mind to attain knowledge. Job acknowledged, *"No mortal comprehends its worth; it cannot be found in the land of the living"* (Job 28:13 NIV). The very basis of a need to understand living things is remarkable; and Job's questions were undeniably edifying and revealed that man has a limited knowledge to their natural habitation and to the wealth of wisdom.

Job's narrative accentuated awareness of character in his natural surroundings. His first quest was directed to "the depth and the sea." The word "depth" in this phrase references a depth beneath the surface of the earth and the sea with similar magnitude. Likewise, the depth and the sea both refuted, *"It is not in me"* (Job 28:14 NIV). They were not familiar with the origin of wisdom and understanding. Then, the search for wisdom was inquired of "death and destruction." They overtly affirmed of their awareness of the fame of wisdom and acknowledged that it was "only God" who had the knowledge of the place and the existence of wisdom and grace.

The response of *"gold and silver"* was profound, they confessed that they had no evidence to the origin of wisdom. The value of these minerals in society is related to the possession of wealth. Gold and silver accepted a self-effacing attitude of their appraisal to be extremely limited to the wisdom of God. Job revealed that wealth comes from the earth and wisdom cannot be bought, for the fear of the Lord is wisdom. *"It cannot be bought with the finest gold, nor can its price be weighed out in silver"* (Job 28:15 NIV).

Another scripture says that wisdom is more precious than rubies and nothing you desire can compare with her (Proverbs 8:11). It cannot be bought with gold or silver (Job 28:15). The psalmist declared that the fear of the Lord, which is godly wisdom, is more precious than gold and is sweeter than honey (Psalm 19:10). King David proclaimed that the Law from the mouth of God is more precious to him than thousands of pieces of gold and silver (Psalm 119:72). The king Solomon stated that *"Wisdom is good with an inheritance: and by it there is profit to them that see the sun. For wisdom is a defense, and money is a defense: but the excellency of knowledge is, that wisdom giveth life to them that have it"* (Ecclesiastes 7:11-12 KJV).

The narrative of Job's story revealed that in his supposition he had to advise himself. The notion of advising "oneself" is in relation to the counsel of the wisdom of God (Job 28:24). Job was humbled by the overwhelming truth as he analyzed his basic thoughts that related to the natural effects. In his account, Job referenced that the truth of wisdom had been hidden from the eyes of the human mind. He highlighted that true wisdom was also oblivious to the birds of the air. Job's statements do propose that it is God alone who has the capability to see to the ends of the earth and it is God who possesses all insight of things pertaining to the heavens (Job 28:22). His fascination of the origination of wisdom correlates to my curiosity, and it is still relevant today.

In my studies, wisdom has stimulated questions that play a part of vast oceans. The wisdom they possess in their natural occurrences and to the extent that at a surge the seas will rise and fall. Unfortunately, no human force could halt these activities. In other events, environmentalists seem to give their reports of saving the planet from coming destruction without the consideration of God who is the source of all life. The misrepresentation of all the natural perplexity is revealed in the wisdom of God. The scripture says that it is God who gave the wind its weight and apportioned out the waters by measure. It is God who decreed for rain and a way for the thunder.

Many scientists are still in wonder of the marvel of the world today as they try to understand the weather. Detailed research has identified that the moon and the ocean tide are responsive to nature.

There was a documentary aired that tried to associate the phases of the moon to the ocean, they filmed evidence of the high tide and the low tide waters that showed the responsibility of gravity in relative response to the phases of the moon. They explained that a school of sea creatures surfaced to feed at different times naturally. This was amazing to see that the various sea creatures acted in awareness of the tide phases. Their wisdom to feed was specified by their species and sizes. Their behavior patterns in relation to the phases of the moon portrayed God's wisdom.

First, they filmed the smaller fishes and the crawling shrimp that surfaced to feed at the phase of low tide. Then, at the phase of high tide, the bigger creatures like the sharks and whales swam up to beaches to eat. The phases of the moon are in comparison to these occurrences. At a low tide all the small creatures receded, however, if they were disobedient to retreat, they became lunch for the larger creatures. They showed that smaller fishes and shrimp became lunch for the sharks and dolphins. It was informative regarding the adaptation of nature to the wonders of God.

Another phenomenon is during fall season when the trees surrender their leaves to prepare for the winter. Then in turn after the winter season ends, the trees' compliance to bear leaves and fruits is amazing. The perpetual cycle from year to year never ceases to amaze me as the very trees of past times just conform to Mother Nature. The snowflakes are another fascination that I often wonder how they determine their interludes and the science behind their capability to rain showers of ice. The list goes on as I marvel at the wisdom of the moon to hide until the evenings and the constant changes of its phases. The Bible says that the moon is for signs and seasons (Genesis 1:14).

Have you ever thought of the reason why some nations have four seasons in a year while, other nations only have two? Well, these thoughts have prompted the search for answers and the story of Job is full of wisdom prompted by questions like this.

THE CURIOSITY OF JOB

The Intervention of God's Wisdom

There are many stories that exist that can relate to the amazing intervention of wisdom. However, I would like to refer to some that I found intriguing in the word of God. These examples are concerning birds and animals; their capacity to possess an intellectual character is profound. Though their wisdom is a source of the divine creativity of the Father God, it is noticeable in all types of creatures on this earth.

The book of Job primarily describes a few attributes of the wisdom of God as he curiously explores the behavioral patterns of the birds. In his mention of the eagle for instance, he asked a question pertaining to where the bird receive its wisdom. Interestingly, it is said that the eagle is a highly intelligent bird. An Explorer tells a story of how the female bird would make her nest high in the mountainous areas and she would abide on the rock. From her strong place she seeks her meal as her eyes behold her prey from afar off. They say that her teaching skill for her young to fly is to push it off the peak of the rock then, as the young eagle free falls for some distance, she flies ahead and scoops it up to safety. Usually, she does this a few times as practice, until the young learns the art of flying. This is amazing to see.

The proud peacock is another bird to watch in amazement. The Peacock is among the most fascinating and beautiful creatures on the earth. Their prideful attitude is significant, and their goodly wings portray the adequate wisdom given by the Lord. Scientists say that the male peacocks roost in trees, while the peahens are hidden under shrubbery. The peahen scrapes holes in the ground and nests, and her wings are used to warn the eggs in the dust. Then, she would leave her eggs in the earth unprotected; she never considers that her young ones may be crushed by other wild animals. This act displays her confidence in a remarkable way. Funny it can be likened to trusting in the Lord with all your heart and leaning not on your own wisdom and understanding (Proverbs 3:5-6).

My curiosity of another peculiar bird is the ostrich. These birds usually lay gigantic eggs. Scientists tell us that each egg is about six inches long. The male and the female ostrich both have received the wisdom from God that causes them to take turns sitting on their eggs until they are hatched. They say this is a lengthy process which lasts for over 42 days. Also, they lay over 50 eggs at one time, which is incredible.

I have determined that only the Lord knows the answer to why the hawk flies and spread its wings towards the south. All these statistics of the wisdom of a bird's life are mentioned in (Job 39). You can read this to understand God's plan of wisdom, for His creation.

> *"They that wait upon the Lord shall renew their strength; they shall mount up with wings as eagles; they shall run and not be weary, they shall walk and not faint."*
> (Isaiah 40:31 KJV)

The promise of the Lord to elevate your faith in Him is evident as your trust in Jesus Christ and wait for Him. The Bible used the analogy of the eagle's wings to illustrate that you will mount up with the wings like the eagle (Isaiah 40:31). Therefore, as a faithful believer, you shall have wisdom and knowledge in comparison to the eagles and the tenacity to dare to fly high into the unknown places with the Lord. Furthermore, a biblical principle of walking in great tenacity and strength is for those who trust in the Lord to be encouraged. The prophet declared that, you will hear a voice behind you saying, *"This is the way, walk in it, whenever you turn to the right hand or whenever you turn to the left hand"* (Isaiah 30:21 NKJV).

The book of Proverbs tells us, *"Happy is the man that findeth wisdom, and the man that getteth understanding"* (Proverbs 3:13). I submit that wisdom can be classified as an essential commodity of life. The gift of wisdom and understanding is a spiritual gift that cannot be revealed without the Holy Spirit and it is subject to the determination of all nature of spiritual understanding.

Chapter 11
The Treasures of Wisdom

"The fear of the Lord is the beginning of wisdom: A good understanding have all they that do his commandments: his praise shall endureth for ever."
(Psalms 111:10 KJV)

The scripture declared that wisdom is the principle of all the fear or reverence to God. Another translation says, *"The fear of the Lord is the beginning of wisdom; and all who follow His precepts have good understanding. To him belongs eternal praise"* (Psalm 112:1 NIV). This tells us, "Blessed is the man or woman who finds great delight in His commands. His children will be mighty in their land and the generation of the upright will be blessed. Wealth and riches are in his house and righteousness endures forever."

Who can explain God's wisdom? (Roman 11:33)

The Apostle Paul questioned the integrity of wisdom. He found that through his intellectual knowledge that God's wisdom was beyond infinite understanding. This treasure of wisdom is inexhaustible. The meaning of the word "wisdom" is related to the knowledge of God and can be applied to the plans of God. Wisdom is how God accomplished all things in His way of goodness, without error. Spiritual wisdom is the complexity of His riches that causes our spiritual eyes to be open and our spiritual ears to be alert with a receptive heart to the voice of God.

The writer of the book of Ecclesiastes, was not specified but the Sages say that the individual must have had a vision, and experience seeking the treasure of wisdom. The writer said, *"I saw every work of God, I concluded that one cannot discover the work which has been done under the sun. Even though a person laboriously seeks, he will not discover; and even if the wise person claims to know, he cannot discover"* (Ecclesiastes 8:17 NASB). The Sages say it could have been Solomon, but it is unverified.

The prophet Isaiah explained that it was the Lord who taught farmers the wisdom and understanding of producing crops. God gave the Israelite crop growers the treasure of the wisdom of seasons and times of various crops. For example, the barley and wheat seasons where they develop and ripen are in the season of Passover and Yom Kippur. Isaiah proclaimed, *"The Lord Almighty, whose plan is wonderful, whose wisdom is magnificent"* (Isaiah 28:26-29 NIV).

In those times, mankind was mostly agriculturalists or fishermen and they could relate to nature. The Sages say it is the reason why during Jesus' ministry He taught with reference to reflect the wisdom of creation. Jesus referred to nature as He said, *"Look at the birds of the air, for they neither sow nor reap, nor gather into barns; yet your heavenly Father feeds them."* Then, in another verse He asked His followers to *"Consider the lilies of the field, how they grow: they neither, toil nor spin; and yet I say to you that even Solomon in all his glory was not arrayed like one of these"* (Matthew 6:26-29 NKJV). Jesus understood that they could relate to these parables and recognized that His wisdom was divine. He needed them to rely on God for the rain and the provision of their increased harvest. They should not be anxious for food, for the birds were worth less than people, yet God fully provides for them.

According to the scriptures, *"Thou knowest not what is the way of the spirit, nor how the bones do grow in the womb of her that is with child: even so you knoweth not the works of God who maketh all"* (Ecclesiastes 11:5 KJV). The writer declared that the treasure of wisdom is hidden in God, in the secret developmental stages of the birth of the child. Jewish Scholars state that this phrase in Ecclesiastes was regarding the birth of the child within Mary's womb (John 3:6). Moreover, in a commentary they say that this verse refers to the intricate works of God which could ordain all our wisdom and knowledge to details of how things work, and in all aspects the ways of God are above or higher than our ways (Isaiah 55:8 KJV).

According to the book of Genesis, Noah had the ability to discern the times and seasons and God gave him the wisdom strategically to build an ark for the purpose of judgment. Noah's walk was in obedience to God, and there was no one willing to help with the building of the ark. He had to endure the mockers and scoffers who said it was foolish to prepare for rain. In those days the people never saw rain and they did not have the wisdom of the outpouring of God's glory. However, the day came when the water of rain lifted the ark above the flood. The Sages say that it was a paradox and Noah could not rescue anyone. They say it is likened to the glory of God which elevates the true vessels of His kingdom.

The scripture tells us that after the crucifixion, there were two of Jesus' disciples that decided to go back to the village the very day, Jesus rose from the grave. As they were in route on their journey, they began to discuss the scenario of what transpired over that week. Abruptly, Jesus came near to join them as He continued the journey with them. He inquired of their conversation to understand why they seemed disheartened. One of the relatives named Cleopas replied by asking Jesus if He was a stranger in town and did not know what was happening presently in the city. Then, they correlated the events and the revelations and prophecy of Jesus of Nazareth.

Afterwards, Jesus responded by revealing that Messiah was within all the writings of the Torah from the days of Moses to the crucifixion, and He explained, "It was deemed for Him to suffer and die". Eventually, their destination was approaching and they urged Him to stay within their home for the night. The Bible says when they sat at the dinner table, Jesus took the bread and blessed it and He broke it. Immediately their eyes were opened and Jesus vanished (Luke 24: 13-31).

Jesus knew their customs and did the blessing of the family meal. The Sages say that it was unusual for a stranger to bless the Jewish meal. Therefore, when their hearts were burning, they overlooked the wisdom of the actions of Jesus and the prompting of the Holy Spirit. Nevertheless, Jesus caused their spiritual senses to be opened and then He vanished. The point Jesus wanted to make was whether you see Him or not, He is there all the time. He will open your eyes by faith to see the invisible, to remind us that His wisdom and discernment is vital to our walk with God. This story encourages the believer to comprehend that the treasures of knowledge can be invisible, for the Lord is forever present and He will protect you. His provision is available even when you are not conscious of His presence.

"For faith is the ability to see the invisible and to believe the impossible." The scripture says, "Moses by faith forsook Egypt, not fearing the wrath of the king. He endured as seeing Him who is invisible" (Hebrew 11:27). This is encouraging to know that wisdom and understanding of God will activate your intimacy with the Lord Jesus Christ.

Apostle Paul pronounced that there was no figuring out God's wisdom and he could not understand wisdom, there was no human that could explain the wisdom of God. As Paul proclaimed, *"Oh, the dept of the riches of the wisdom and knowledge of Go! How searchable is his judgements, and his paths beyond tracing out! Who has known the mind of the Lord? Or who has been his counsellor? Who has ever given to God, that God should repay them?"* (Roman 11:33 NIV)

Wisdom and Understanding

"The fear of the Lord is the beginning of knowledge: but fools despise wisdom and instruction."
(Proverbs 1:7 NIV)

The evidence of a relationship with God is prayer and the cultivation of wisdom. Some of the sermons of wisdom were highlighted in the prayers of King Solomon. In his youth, when he became aware of the task of the ruler of the nation of Israel, God gave Solomon material wealth and spiritual wisdom for he had only requested the wisdom of God. Jewish Historians say that Solomon was the wisest king that ever lived.

Moses could be known as the "Sagest" prophet that functioned in the divine revelation of God. Moses' encounters with the Lord resulted in his declaration that *"the secret things belong to the Lord our God, but the things revealed belong to us and to our children forever, that we may follow all the words of this law"* (Deuteronomy 29:29 NIV). This phrase meant that all the inevitabilities of this life are determined by God and it is in His power to make known only those things that He did not desire to be concealed from mankind (Deuteronomy 29:29). Moses was a servant of God, and the prophets understood that it was God who chose them as His mouthpiece. The prophets in those days were known for their prophetic utterances to Israel. The prophets Jeremiah, Daniel, Samuel and Isaiah were among those that operated in divine wisdom. Others chosen in Israel were King David, Joseph the son of Jacob, Joshua, Samson and Solomon. However, the king Solomon walked in divine wisdom for some of his reign. Ultimately, the greatest of them all is Jesus Christ. In fact, the Bible says that Jesus was anointed to function in all the levels of divine wisdom and knowledge of God.

The prophet Daniel was among the children known to possess a character of no fault or sin, and he was well favored of God, skillful in all wisdom, and in knowledge. Daniel understood that the availability of wisdom resulted from praying and fasting. Therefore, on one occasion Daniel fasted for ten days and he petitioned for his desire to be undefiled before the Lord. His patience to wait portrayed his divine wisdom. One of the benefits of prayer and fasting manifested in his spiritual knowledge and discernment. God used dreams and visions to communicate with Daniel after he prayed and gave him answers. The Bible tells us that Daniel's response to the pharaoh's dream was a prime example of the wisdom of God that resulted in the saving grace even of the prophets of Babylon.

A Godly fast involves the truth concerning the standard of a fast according to God. The prophet Isaiah was explicit of the Lord's chosen fast and he revealed that it was not limited to the works of God, but conditional to the reflection of wisdom and understanding towards the things of God. The scripture tells us that God will hear and answer our prayers according to our understanding of His truth. God saw that the children of Israel were off track in their belief and Isaiah prophesied God's requirements of the fast by saying, *"Is not this the fast that I have chosen? To loose the bands of wickedness, to undo the heavy burdens, and to let the oppressed go free"* (Isaiah 58:6-8 KJV). This particular verse of scripture made me aware that the fasting God requires of His followers is for a set period of time which in Hebrew they are known as "moedim." The Jewish people would assemble at these specific times on their calendar, year by year to fast and pray. Moreover, these occasions are set apart times to seek the will of God and to remember what He had done for them throughout their generations.

The leadership to Joshua was transferred by Moses according to the Lord's command. He received an anointing for divine wisdom and the courage to carry the Israelites into the promise land. During his leadership Joshua defeated Canaan in battle. Moreover, there were times when Joshua experienced a setback in war and the Bible says that he inquired of the Lord. In other words, Joshua sought the Lord for divine wisdom and the Lord responded to Joshua prayers. He revealed that there was sin in the midst of the camp. Joshua received the revelation knowledge of someone amongst them that hid an idol belonging to their enemy within the camp. As a result, the judgment of God was allowing their army to be ca defeated because of the sin. Then, God commanded Joshua to destroy that man in order to reverse their defeat to victory. This story reveals that one person's sin can affect a whole nation concerning the judgment of God.

The Sages say that it was significant in the dilemma of Abraham and Haggai. Abraham casting out Haggai and her son was vital to the promise of Isaac. Haggai feared the unknown and the plight of losing her son Ishmael. In the book of Genesis, it tells us that she received a promise from God, and He spoke to Haggai that He had a great plan for Ishmael. Therefore, she could not leave the child under the bushel to die. She obeyed and returned to pick up her promise, for it was vital for her to have faith in the God of Abraham to see the promise. Haggai had to trust God to endure the hardship ahead, for she knew His promise to Sarah, and she saw the evidence that it came to pass. Her faith in God's wisdom must have grown because God performed miracles.

The ability to comprehend God's plan for our future is unpredictable. God has great plans for us and our family, though you cannot comprehend it. Haggai's story was written as an encouragement to others who would walk this path in life. By faith, the Lord will open the eyes of our understanding as we call out to Him for "Help!" In Psalms 91, David's prophetic insight is an encouragement to the believer, it says. *"For He shall give His angels charge over you, to keep you in all your ways"* (Psalms 91:11 NKJV). To understanding the concept of the word of God the apostle John declared, *"For whatsoever is born of God overcomth the world: and this is the victory that overcometh the world, even our faith. This is he that came by water and blood, even Jesus Christ; not by water only, but by water and blood. And it is the spirit that beareth witness, because the Spirit is Truth"* (1 John 5:4-6 KJV).

The function of the Holy Spirit leads us into the prayer that reinforces the wisdom and revelation of various circumstances. The Lord uses dreams and visions to enlighten our spiritual intelligence to things happening behind the scenes. *"Now unto him that is able to do exceedingly, abundantly, above all that we ask or think, according to the power that worketh in us"* (Ephesians 3:20 KJV).

In one of the visions that the prophet Jeremiah received, he declared, *"He has made the earth by His power, He has established the world by His wisdom; and has stretched out the heavens at His discretion"* (Jeremiah 10:12-13 NKJV). King David revealed an identical disclosure in his writings of the divine wisdom of God and His wisdom as the Creator. David declared, *"O Lord, how manifold are thy works! In wisdom has thou made them all"* (Psalm 104:24 KJV). The Psalmist Asaph also acknowledged that the wisdom of the Lord is in the works of God. He concluded that God is in control of the wonders of the world as well as the Israelite people. The observation that Asaph described was an association and reaction of the waters, seas, and the clouds, as the skies that send out sounds were likened to the thunder and lightning in the heavens and the shaking of the earth (Psalm 77:19).

A very popular scripture that most believers rehearse is the phrase, *"Surely the Lord God does nothing, unless He reveals His secret to His servants the prophets"* (Amos 3:7 NKJV). The prophet Amos surely was recognizing an elite people, he referred to those which are called the servants of God in relation to their experience with the benefit of the wisdom of God. The basis of the criteria for the wisdom of God, to know the secret things of God, is given by the Holy Spirit. According to the word of God it comes with seeking the Lord with all your heart, for it is a gift. In other words, for the believer who faithfully and genuinely walks in the fear of God, there will be nothing that would happen to you by surprise.

The apostle Paul, in his teachings, talked about the immaturity and unskillfulness of men. He admonished the believers to seek after the Lord with their desire for much wisdom and knowledge.

> *"For everyone that useth milk is unskillful in the word of righteousness: for he is a babe. (He lacks wisdom) But strong meat belongeth to them that are of full age, even those who by reason of use have their senses exercised to discern both good and evil."*
> (Hebrew 5:13-14 KJV)

King David had a humble heart, and the Bible says that the Lord loved David as a friend. For this reason, David desired for his sons to walk in right standing with God and not make the same mistakes he did. His son Solomon subsequently became the king of Israel after David's death. Moreover, the Lord chose Solomon to be king, and his father David knew that there were insights he had to impart to his son about the Lord. Solomon began his kingship with the right motive, but he began to increase in pride and disobedience. David instructed Solomon to build the house for the Lord, yet Solomon took his time. The Bible tells us that Solomon first built himself a house (1 Kings 3:1). The Lord identified the heart of Solomon, as He warned him of his own agenda.

The prayer of David to the Lord for Solomon kingship:

> *"Give the king Your judgments, O God, and Your righteousness to the king's son. He will judge Your people with righteousness, and Your poor with judgment and justice."*
> (Psalms 72:1-2 NKJV)

The Two Hebrew Midwives

> *"The heart of the prudent acquires knowledge, and the ear of the wise seeks knowledge. A man's gift makes room for him, and brings him before great men."*
> (Proverbs 18:15-16 NKJV)

Israel was still in the land of Egypt after the death of Joseph, when a new pharaoh began his reigned. The Bible tells us that the previous pharaohs were aware of the wisdom of the Hebrew Abraham and they acknowledged Joseph as a Hebrew man. However, this new pharaoh who came many years after, was not aware of Joseph's wisdom and contribution to the survival of the Egyptians. Therefore, when his counselors came and spoke against the Hebrew people, the pharaoh became attentive to their growth and inventions in the land. He began to take their ungodly advice of how to disintegrate the Jewish community. As a result, the pharaoh used his authority to decree death to the Hebrew boys up to two years of age.

The pharaoh called for assistance from two Hebrew midwives that were in Egypt. In their dilemma the scripture noted that these Hebrew midwives were honorable and God-fearing women (Exodus 1:13). Their names were Shiphrah (Shifra) and Puah. These women elected to disobey the king's commands, for their actions portrayed the gift of wisdom in the knowledge of God's word, *"Thou shall not kill"* (Exodus 20:13). They honored God and risked their lives for many Hebrew infants. God knew the crisis and their courage of faith, and in their defense He rewarded their heroic boldness. The Bible says that the Lord established their household and they became matriarchs of the nation of Israel. He caused the children of Israel to build houses for the two midwives (I King 11:38). The Sages propose that one of these women, whose name was Shihrah, had been identified with Jochebed and she was the mother of Moses. They say that the terrible plot of the Egyptian pharaoh made her secure Moses in the basket to preserve his divine destiny.

The Act of a Woman

In the Bible, there was another wise woman mentioned, and her actions were motivated by her wisdom. Her name was not mentioned in this story, but she was called the woman of Abel-Beth-Maacah (2 Samuel 20). Throughout Israel, she was known to live a peaceable and faithful life. The story described the day that Joab the captain of host of the King David's army, besieged the city of Abel. The city was surrounded with the army and there were soldiers battering the wall of her city intending to make it crumble under Joab's command. The Sages say that it was impossible for anyone to leave to get supplies for their families.

The woman was aware of the scenario, and she understood that someone needed to save the children and the few men of that city. In the face of danger, she called out to Joab and inquired of the purpose for their besiegement. In response, Joab told her that there was a man called Sheba, the son of Bichri, who was hiding in her city. This man, Sheba, sought to begin a civil war against the king David, and Joab requested that Sheba be delivered to the king to be punished. The Bible tells us that she bartered peace between her city and Joab, in exchange they threw the head of the rebel Sheba over the wall. Her wisdom and advice saved her city from destruction and she acquired peace instead of violence; her city was justified.

The Hebrew Sages say the woman was knowledgeable of the laws of God concerning wars. Moses commanded, *"When you approach a city to fight against it, you shall offer it terms of peace. And if it agrees to make peace with you and opens to you, then all the people who are found in it shall become your forced labor and serve you"* (Deuteronomy 20:10 NASB). They say that her wisdom was likened to the woman of "Proverbs 31:26" for her persuasiveness and knowledge of the word of God produces a mouth full of wisdom. In the book of James, her wisdom would be linked to the peacemaker (James 3:17). *"Blessed are the peacemakers for they will be called the children of God"* (Matthew 5:9 NIV).

King Solomon wrote that wisdom is more valuable than weapons of war, and that this woman was much superior to Joab's weapons (Ecclesiastes 9:18). A Jewish scholar commentary stated that the woman's astuteness can be compared to the wisdom of Abraham when he came before God to plead for Sodom.

"He that dwelleth in the secret place of the Most High (God) shall abide under the shadow of the Almighty."
(Psalm 91:1KJV)

All these stories and many more testimonies reveal that when people seek council from the Lord they are endowed with such wisdom to overcome an adversary.

Solomon's Wisdom Distorted

One of my favorite phrases in the Bible is of Solomon asking God for an understanding heart to judge all Israel (1 Kings 3:9). The story relates to the intricacy of Solomon's life at the crowning of his kingship, he was very immature and unskillful in the beginning. The Jewish culture of Solomon's parents should have entailed Solomon's knowledge of the principles of God that Jews follow according to their prophet Moses. His father (David) regaled in the counsel of the Lord and Solomon had an example of obedience to God's laws. The fundamental key in his prayer was for his heart as he demonstrated the scripture that says, "It is out of the heart that flows all the issues of life" (Proverbs 4:23).

At this stage of Solomon's kingship, he recognized that with God there is a covenant inheritance of wisdom. The writer tells us that after the death of David, Solomon prayed to the Lord for guidance in the affairs of the kingdom. Maybe, Solomon as a young man recognized his inadequacy to his assignment of being the king of Israel. He asked for wisdom and an understanding heart to judge the people righteously and discernment to differentiate the good from evil. His prayer for the wisdom of the Lord made the Lord respond with wisdom, wealth, and a long life as a covenant of mercy and faithfulness. From the Hebrew perspective, the Sages say that Solomon was one of the greatest kings that ever lived.

They say that King Solomon exceeded in abundant wisdom and his fame became known throughout the nations of the world (1 Kings 4:29-31). At this juncture it could be said the Solomon had spiritual and natural wisdom to allow wealth. The Sages say that he possessed business and trade skills to fulfill the building of the temple for God. He gave wise counsel to the nation and abroad. There is an important principle of the law that governs our expectation for living a long life with wealth and prosperity (I Kings 3:4-13). *"With long life I will satisfy him and show him my salvation"* (Psalm 91:16 NIV).

The covenant promise of God to the people of Israel and David was evident in Solomon's situation. The Lord promised David that his seed shall sit on the throne of the house of Israel forever (2 Samuel 7:16). The Bible tells us that King David prayed for Solomon that the Lord would be obverse or primary in all his affairs. This was David's caution to Solomon, that he would continually walk upright with the Lord. The word "upright" refers to "a straight path," it can also refer to "never wavering in doubt or unbelief." In the experiences that David had, he could have given his son great advice to the requirement of a perfect heart towards God. The knowledge and counsel David provided was great insight to becoming a great king. Solomon understood that it was required of every Israelite king to walk in right standing with God or in other words, "to walk upright." Solomon had the facts for successful leadership. In another statement, David declared that the nature of the Lord is to search out the hearts of men and He has the discernment of all their thoughts and imaginations. David warned Solomon to never forsake the Lord, or he would then be cast away from God forever (1 Chronicles 28:9). Solomon had all the wisdom he needed to be wealthy spiritually, but somehow, he got sidetracked and began to offer sacrifices and burnt incense in the high places. This was something the Lord told the children of Israel not to do. In His mercy, because of His covenant with David, the Lord came in dreams by night to warn Solomon of his disobedience and the consequences of his actions. According to the apostle Paul, *"God is no respecter of persons"* (Romans 2:11). It resulted in Solomon's demise as he ignored his warning of the Lord and his kingdom was divided into two.

Chapter 12
The Ungodly Wisdom

"Blessed is the man that walk not in the counsel of the ungodly, but he delights himself in the Lord"
(Psalm 1:1).

A clear description of wisdom is identified as the divine counsel of God and the ungodly counsel. The theological term for "ungodly wisdom" is defined as "the denial of godly wisdom." The Sages suggest that ungodly wisdom alludes to the suppressing of the truth of God's word. Moreover, ungodly wisdom can be an indication of an evil perception which leads to behaviors of a destructive lifestyle. This subject can also be associated with a natural wisdom. A Hebraic Scholar commented that ungodly wisdom is a result of a pessimistic approach to wisdom, it inevitably renders to a self-exaltation and an idolatrous way of life.

On some occasions, Jesus addressed His followers on the topic of ungodly wisdom. In the New Testament, He instructed them on how to behave in their ministry and to discern the ungodly. Jesus declared to His disciples, "There were some amongst Him who had characteristics of a wicked heart." This would have pointed to his friend Judas at the time. In another teaching, Jesus used metaphors with His disciples saying to be as wise as a serpent (Matthew 10:16). Then, He warned them of the dubious encounters that they might experience while they were being sent out. Jesus also described the disciples as sheep among wolves.

The word of God affirms that the serpent is a representation of evil wisdom and it must be contended with and overcome. Satan, who is known as the devil, does exist and his dogma is crafty and inevitable. Jesus, in His teaching, used the relevance of the serpent to elevate the disciples' awareness. The word "serpent" is likened to "the character of a traitor, a liar, and a troublemaker." The Bible detailed the description of the serpent as one that was more subtle and crafty than any other beast of the field (Genesis 3:1). Scientists have clarified that a serpent's nature is to induce fear in the sense to gain respect from human beings. Jesus also used the wolf metaphor to liken their characters to that of the sheep because He was aware of the plots against Him. In scientific research, I found that the wolf is described as an animal with traits of keen instinct and intelligence. A wolf will attack its prey with a speed compared to a car.

In a sermon Jesus rebuked the religious leaders and again He used the metaphor of the viper to warn the Pharisees and the scribes of being hypocrites. He told them, "They put aside the commandments of God to observe human traditions." In other words, Jesus told them, "You lay aside the commands of God, and you hold on to the traditions of men" (Mark 7:9). The Pharisees did not believe that Jesus Christ was the Messiah or that He was sent from God. Jesus knew their cultural belief and their Jewish history caused them to deny the immorality of the soul, the resurrection from the dead, and the existence of angelic spirits. Therefore, they were plotting and preparing to slay Him behind the scenes. On the other hand, the Sadducees refused to live beyond the Torah, which are the five books written by Moses.

In the same way, the scribes and Pharisees were rebuked by John the Baptist and he called them a "brood of vipers" for they were known to be wicked and unbelieving (Matthew 3:7). In the book of Isaiah, the Lord explained to the prophet that the people were unfaithful to Him. The Lord spoke to Isaiah and said, *"These people come near to me with their mouth and honor me with their lips, but their heart is far from me"* (Isaiah 29:13 NIV). This meant that some of the people had a personality which God deemed as despicable, and their hearts were full of deviousness, dishonesty, and unreliability.

The illustrations of evil or ungodly acts are prominent in the word of God and few were noticeable to catch my attention. They were the ungodly wisdom of King Saul, and the prophet Balaam. The humiliation that David experienced as the servant of God was obviously pure hatred from King Saul. He conducted himself in the craftiness of the serpent (1 Kings 19). The second story was the prophet Balaam and the Israelites (Numbers 22:28). It is inexplicable the great measure of love and creativity that God has invested into human-beings that this story reveals how much sensitivity and intelligence God has placed in animals. The funny part of this story is the donkey's ability to reason compared to Balaam. The donkey's wisdom to discern the situation at that moment seemed more spiritual than its master. Moreover, without his donkey's insight to obey the angel, which was blocking their way, Balaam's spiritual blindness could have resulted in his death. There are other instances where the scriptures highlight animals with a measure of undeniable wisdom such as birds, foxes, lions, and birds, including the serpent.

King Saul operated in both categories of wisdom, and in the book of Samuel, it is revealed that Saul did fear God to an extent. However, he often rebelled against God's ordinances and revealed his unbelief. At times, Saul showed honor to Samuel's counsel and at other times he disobeyed God. The children of Israel conquered lands and the Lord commanded Moses to tell the people not to practice the sins of the heathens. Therefore, all witches and people that practice witchcraft must be put to death. According to Moses, *"Thou shalt not suffer a witch to live"* (Exodus 22:18). In fact, God in His wisdom knew that those who performed such actions would practice evil against His children of Israel. Saul understood the Hebraic laws, and this was instructed to the kings, the priests, and the children of Israel that a witch shall not be kept alive. According to the Bible, King Saul was knowledgeable of the word of God concerning witches and wizards. It is revealed that Saul, in his beginnings of kingship, did execute most of the witches that practiced such atrocities against others. However, Saul never pursued those that fled into hiding (1 Samuel 28:3).

In one scenario, Saul was distressed by the Philistines' army and he needed counsel against them in battle. There is no mention of Saul seeking God in true repentance or seeking the Lord through other prophets of his day for counsel. The Bible states that Saul experienced the power of God after meeting the prophet Samuel on one occasion when he travelled through a place to the hills. There he met a group of prophets prophesying and the spirit of God came upon him. Then, he began to prophesy among them (1 Samuel 10:10). However, instead of consulting the prophets of Israel (even though he was acquainted with them), he erred and sought a medium for his consultation.

Way back in the book of Exodus, God warned the Israelites against witchcraft and He called these ungodly acts abominable. In His commands, the Lord spoke to Moses and said, *"Do not defile yourselves by turning to mediums or to those who consult the spirits of the dead. I am the LORD your God"* (Leviticus 19:31 NLT). In another translation it says, *"Regard not them that have familiar spirits, neither seek after wizards, to be defiled by them: I am the LORD your God"* (KJV). The Lord was very explicit on the victory of Israel and the guidelines for their success. Moses rehearsed to the children of Israel in his final days saying, *"When you come into the land which the Lord your God is giving you, you shall not learn to follow the abominations of those nations"* (Deuteronomy 18:9-14 NKJV). All these instructions are still for the children of God today.

King Saul inverted the commands of God and in rebellion he requested to consult with the witch of the city of Endor. The story tells us that the witch recognized that kind of request from the king and she was afraid. It would cost her, her life to do such acts for the king of Israel, and she tried to dissuade him from his request. Nevertheless, Saul resolved to persuade her that her life was not on the line as he avowed never to execute her. Her demonic acts invoked a familiar spirit, which the Bible describes as a familiar sound that arose, likened to the familiar voice of the prophet Samuel. There was no way that a witch could have dwelt in the same room with the prophet Samuel; contrary to our thinking light and darkness cannot dwell together. Samuel would have thrashed the medium. Moreover, the Bible did not say that Saul saw Samuel, but it tells us that the witch described an old man and King Saul cried out to Samuel. The story even says that the spirit rejected Saul and he was devastated. Saul in a state of insanity, and he did exactly what God had forbidden the children of Israel to do. The mention of Saul's condition was so moving that the witch beckoned him to eat something she prepared, and he ate from her hand that night. The following morning King Saul was judged by God and it led to his demise.

As I considered this episode, a simple truth was revealed regarding witchcraft. I saw that God would use the wickedness of man and still reject their sinful actions. According to King David, he recognized that God was everywhere even when he didn't fathom his presence. He declared, *"If I ascend up into the heaven, thou art there: if I make my bed in hell, behold, thou art there"* (Psalm 139:8 KJV). It is forbidden by God to speak to the deceased, for it not natural but it is demonic, for dead relatives to return and speak to the living is impossible. Moreover, the apostle Luke indicated that there was a great gulf that is fixed that divided heaven and hell, and hence, the spirits cannot interact (Luke 16: 19-31).

The lesson here is that God's presence can depart. Therefore, Saul's evil deeds had deprived him of a relationship with the presence of God. God's judgment was predetermined of his integrity and morals. The Bible stated that Saul became insane, and this was the result of the perversion of his reasoning. King Saul was prideful, and it blurred his vision to the work of God. Instead, his entire fixation was the ungodly wisdom that made him afraid of David's popularity and he displayed wickedness, and murderous thoughts towards an innocent young man. He became determined to destroy the new anointed king of Israel for over twenty years and until his death (1 Samuel 18).

> *"There is a way that seems right to a man,*
> *but the end is the way of death."*
> (Proverbs 16:25 NKJV)

In King Solomon's reign, he recognized that there is a path to wisdom. Solomon declared that wisdom and knowledge seemed to propel mankind into the path of righteousness. This path of wisdom would deliberately cause them to shun the ungodly path that leads to destruction. According to Solomon, *"Wisdom will save you from the ways of wicked men whose words are preverse"* (Proverbs 2:12 NIV). The scriptures reference ungodly wisdom to unchaste women. Solomon stated that the divine wisdom of God will save us from the immoral lifestyles and from the promiscuous woman, with her seductive words. For her house will lead down to death and her path to the spirits of death. None who go to her return or attain the path of life (Proverbs 2:12-19).

Wisdom is differentiated into two pathways. One is the path of divine wisdom and the other is the path of foolishness and evil. Divine wisdom leads to a path of success and righteousness as foolish wisdom leads to a path of failure and destruction. In one of Solomon's proverbs, he noted that to walk unwisely is the path of the consequences of destruction. Solomon acknowledged, *"You will walk in the ways of the good and keep to the paths of righteous"* (Proverbs 2:20 NIV). According to the book of Matthew, there is a narrow gate, and there is a broad way that leads to destruction (Matthew 7:13).

In book of Revelation, John asserted that the character of the ungodly is associated with "cowards, unbelievers, the corrupt, murderers, the immoral, those who practice witchcraft, idol worshippers, and all liars." John declared, "Those people shall have their fate in the fiery lake of burning sulfur. This is the second death" (Revelation 21:8 NLT). John warned the believer not to be deceived, for ungodly wisdom is the refusal to trust in God. Evidently, the unsavory behavior entails the second death which is eternal suffering in the lake of fire. This references a spiritual death, Jesus also mentioned this in his sermons as he taught that it is worthless to gain the whole world and lose your soul (Mark 8:36).

In the story of Joseph and the wife of Potiphar, there was no mention of her beauty or name in the scriptures. The Bible tells us that she casted her eyes on Joseph immorally. Perchance, she was thinking it would lure Joseph to her intentional absurd act. The

THE UNGODLY WISDOM

ungodly wife of Potiphar begged him to commit immorality with her. However, the story reveals that a godly man like Joseph was an honest, and he feared God, and it instantly cause him to refuse to be disobedient to his God (Genesis 39:7-10). Joseph's commitment to godliness was his reverential fear of the Lord. His decision landed him in the prison but his faith in God reveals his wisdom. This lesson demonstrates that Joseph's empowerment against the trap of enticement and evil actions.

Balaam's Ungodly Acts

The Israelites took their journey, as God commanded Moses, towards the land of Canaan. They encountered various challenges along their journey and the one that God was very angry about was the children of Amalek. However, the Lord delivered them from all their enemies. In those days, one of their obstacles was the king of Moab. He felt threatened by the children of Israel when he heard their reputation of defeating the other nations on their journey. King Balak heard that the Israelites were outside the plains of Moab and felt intimidated by their army's success. Therefore, he sought for a wise prophet that was famous in his region to come cast a curse over the Israelites. The story tells us that his choice of rescue was the son of Beor, whose name was Balaam. The king sent messengers to bring Balaam to his city, so that he would cause the Moabites to defeat the Israelites.

The flamboyance of Balaam's wisdom was ungodly, for he had personal jealousy against the people of Israel. Hebraic history reveals that Balaam was the grandson of Laban, and like his grandpa, he used divination for the purpose of sorcery. The Sages state that Balak was connected to Abraham's nephew Lot. The desire of Balak to curse the children of Israel also placed him in ungodly wisdom. Balak believed that Balaam could use the divine name of God to achieve his evil agenda. The scripture tells us that Balaam himself said that he heard from God and he was the vessel to do the king's bidding. The king intended to defeat the army of Israel and Balaam purposed in his heart to curse the Israelites in exchange for currency or wealth.

The Bible says that Balaam was warned by God that very night, and he became sidetracked as God instructed him to bless the children of Israel instead. However, Balaam was adept to play the role of the accuser before the Lord and his stubbornness caused his donkey to open his mouth to rebuke him (Numbers 22). It is funny to learn that the donkey spoke three times before his master Balaam retorted. It took Balaam this many times before his eyes were opened, for he had no spiritual insight to the things of God. The message here is that Balaam, on the way to commit sin, could not see with his own eyes, even when God specifically spoke to him. The Sages say that Balaam is a foretelling of "Haman" whose malice and jealousy against the Hebrews drove him to ultimately destroy his own life. This story of Haman is found in the book of Esther. This comparison also reminded me of the "accuser of the brethren," who is the Devil, for he is the father of lies.

The apostle Peter said, *"The way of Balaam, the son of Beor, who loved the wages of unrighteousness"* (2 Peter 2:14-15 NKJV). Balaam had professed God, but there was no evidence written of his good works or his relationship aligned with the God of Israel (Numbers 22:13). The Bible tells us that Balaam tried to curse the children of Israel various times and he was unsuccessful. Balaam, in his quest, tried to manipulate God in exchange for the praises of men. In his desperation, Balaam devised an ungodly plot with the Moabites to cause the people of Israel to behave immorally and fall into sin (Numbers 31:16). The story concluded with Balaam cursing Balak.

This topic is relevant to the church today, as a warning to be in right standing with the Lord. In his teachings, Jesus mentioned ungodly wisdom as he referred to the operation of the spirit of Balaam in the book of Revelation. Jesus spoke to John and declared to the churches that God knew of their ungodly wisdom.

> *"I have a few things against you, because you have there, those who hold the doctrine of Balaam, who taught Balak to*

THE UNGODLY WISDOM

put a stumbling block before the children of Israel, to eat things sacrificed to idols, and to commit sexual immorality."
(Revelation 2:14 NKJV)

Gamaliel's Counsel

In the book of Acts, the third chapter, there was a contention within the council as the High Priest and the elders of the Sanhedrin began to seek death penalty for the apostles. Their ungodly characters are propelled to do harm to the apostles Peter and John. One of the councilors, whose name was Gamaliel was included in the Sanhedrin. Moreover, the Bible described Gamaliel as a priest and a doctor of doctrine, who had legal authority for the Laws. Therefore, he could be considered as a man with like passion of an ungodly intention. The Bible tells us that Gamaliel gave counsel to order the apostles out of their presence so that he could express his opinion against the evil inclination of his fellow priests. The meaning of his name in Hebrew means "God is my reward." The Sages say that peoples' names mean something in the Hebrew language and this rabbi was honored by all people. He was known for taking a lenient view of the Old Testament laws in contrast to his Jewish counterparts (Acts 5:34).

The Sages say that Gamaliel was very influential to his council and he encouraged his fellow councilors to be thoughtful in their dealing with Jesus' followers. He recommended the freedom of Peter and John, and his wise suggestion was accepted by the ungodliness of the others. Gamaliel anticipated the movement would dwindle away if this was not from God. However, if it was the believers' crusade, then the ungodly resistance of the council would reflect to the people that they were against God (Acts 5:38-39). He reminded the council of previous Israelite men that had perished for their teachings.

He spoke about "Theudas," who boasted of himself as somebody and the multitudes began to join themselves to him. Theudas, the historians say, led his followers in a short-lived revolt. These people were slayed, scattered, and brought to nothing as a result (Acts 5:36). After this incident, in the time of census, there arose a man named Judas of Galilee. He got people to follow him and drew away many to believe in him.

Judas was a Jewish leader who led the resistance to the census imposed for Roman taxation purposes by the Province of Judea. He encouraged the Jews not to register and those that did obey the law had their houses burnt and their cattle stolen by his followers. However, he also was killed, and all his followers were scattered.

The councilors took his counsel. They decided to call the disciples and they whipped them, commanded them not to speak in the name of Jesus, and afterwards they let them go. On that occasion, Peter and John's lives were saved by the wise counsel of Gamaliel.

> *"Woe to the rebellious children," saith the Lord, "that take counsel, but not of me; and that cover with a covering, but not of my spirit"*
> (Isaiah 30:1 KJV)

The apostle Paul, who was first identified as Saul of Tarsus, persecuted the children of God after the death and ascension of Jesus Christ. One day as Saul was on the road to Damascus and was plotting an evil or ungodly act against God's people, he had an encounter with the Lord God. Saul was struck blind for three days. After this encounter Saul became Paul, one of the greatest apostles of those times. He was the writer of much of the New Testament of the Bible and his ungodly wisdom transformed to godly wisdom (Acts 22:3). Jewish historians say that Paul was a great historian of the laws of God and the Old Testament which enabled him to present Jesus Christ as the one who fulfilled the laws of God and the prophets (Matthew 5:17). Paul acknowledged his zealousness in wrongdoing towards God's chosen people. Moreover, he declared that Jesus is the Messiah of the Jewish people and the world. I submit that one encounter with God can change everything!

THE UNGODLY WISDOM

The apostle Paul was an educated man and he possessed professional credentials although he was misled by his astuteness. It took the Holy Spirit transforming Paul to convert his mindset. After this, Paul began his ministry and wherever he went he preached, *"The kingdom of God is at hand"* (Mark 1:15 KJV). Paul also began to experience opposition from men during his ministry and he accredited that this wisdom was not of God. So, he began to teach the people how to identify ungodly wisdom.

The story was told of the wisdom of a woman in the book of Acts. It could be interpreted as ungodly wisdom because, she was possessed by the spirit of divination. One day as the apostles entered a city, she began to cry out aloud saying, *"These men are the servants of the Most High God!"* She spoke truthfully, however, this was not godly wisdom because she was depraved. The Apostle Paul discerned her plight and he responded in wisdom. His righteous anger made him cast out the demons in an act of deliverance. There was another incident where the apostle Paul discerned that there was a witch in their midst called Bar-Jesus; he detached himself from the counterfeit spirit and rebuked the demon (Acts 13:4-12).

In his writings Paul admonished the believer not to be ignorant of the spiritual gifts of God. He suggests that the Gentiles who were once involved in idolatry should be aware of the spirit of ungodliness. Paul stated, *"No man speaking by the spirit of God would ever deny that Jesus Christ is the Lord."* He explained that the Holy Spirit is the distributor of the special abilities to every man, to some is given the spirit of wisdom, to another the word of knowledge. Paul encouraged them to essentially test the spirits to ensure that they align with the Word of God (1 Corinthians 12:1-11). The scripture says, *"Through desire a man, having separated himself, seeketh and intermeddleth with all wisdom"* (Proverbs 18:1 KJV). It also tells us, *"Cursed be the man that trusteth in man, and maketh flesh his arm, and whose heart departeth from the Lord"* (Jeremiah 17:6 KJV). Another verse of scripture says, *"Put not your trust in princes, nor in the son of man, in whom there is no help"* (Psalms 146:3 KJV).

Chapter 13
The Distinction of the Imprudent

The Bible presents the unwise man's characteristics as the actions of a fool. Their behavior is noted as foolishness with no remorse. The Bible also states that a person who does not act wisely is not following the warnings and requirements of God. They are lacking infinite wisdom and can be in the category of an enemy of God. It is so easy for such a person to act wickedly.

The psalmist David declared, the fool says in his heart, "there is no God". They are corrupt, their deeds are vile and there is not one who does good. The scriptures say, "The Lord looks down from the heaven on the sons of men to see if there are any who understand, any who seek God" (Psalm 14:2).

Jesus addressed this subject and told his followers, *"Everyone who hears these words of mine, and does not do them will be like a foolish man, who built his house on the sand"* (Matthew 7:26 NKJV). In another teaching, He made emphasis of the rich man and his folly, for the day came for his judgment and God said to him, "You fool! This very night your life will be demanded from you" (Luke 12:20 NIV). The apostle was relaying the necessity of having your wisdom and wealth in God, rather than being wise and ungodly.

The apostle Paul, in his message declared, "Let no one deceive himself. If anyone thinks to be wise in this age, let him become a fool that he may become wise (1 Corinthians 3:18 NKJV). Worldly wisdom could be misleading in comparison to the wisdom of God which would lead to righteous living.

The Bible tells us, "It is better for a poor man or humble man, who walks with integrity than a fool whose lips are perverse or stubborn" (Proverbs 19:1).

Here are some thoughts on this topic, according to the Bible, that I found intriguing:

- A fool is unwise and lacks the sense of judgment.
- A fool is a person that turns away from truth and suppresses it for unrighteousness.
- A foolish man is wise in his own eyes; and will reject advice whether it is spiritual or natural.
- A fool is wicked in their heart.
- A fool behaves proudly and idly.
- A fool's mission is to repeatedly behave in sinful acts and find it funny.
- A fool slanders other people.
- A fool tries to lead other people down dark paths.
- Fools rush into danger without having wise preparation.
- Fools have no interest in thoughtfulness, they desire only air their own opinions.
- A fool acts insecurely and it leads him to disgrace, dishonor and scandalous behavior that bring contempt (Proverbs 18:2-3).
- "A fool vent all his feelings, but a wise man holds them back" (Proverbs 29:11 NKJV).
- "A proverb in the mouth of a fool is as useless as a paralyzed leg".
- "Doing wrong is fun for a fool, but living wisely brings pleasure to the sensible.
- *"Wisdom of the prudent is to give thought to their ways, but the folly of fools is deception"* (Proverbs 14:8 NIV).
- *"Fools mock at making amends for sin, but goodwill is found among the upright"* (Proverbs 14:8-10).
- *"A fool's lips enter into contention, and mouth calls for blows"* (Proverbs 18:8 NKJV).
- *"It is as sport to a fool to do mischief, but a man of understanding has wisdom"* (Proverbs 10:23 KJV).
- *"Trusting a fool to convey a message is like cutting off one's feet or drinking poison!"* (Proverbs 26:6 NLT).

THE DISTINCTION OF THE IMPRUDENT

- When the storm has swept by, the wicked are gone, but the righteous stand firm forever" (Proverbs 10:25 NIV).

Hebrew scholars note that there are twenty-two statements in Proverbs referring to the rudiments of an unwise person. They make the comparison of the Hebrew alphabet where there are twenty-two letters. They determined that there is no word like "coincidence" found in the Hebrew language, it is beyond man's understanding.

The Bible enumerates the warning signs of a foolish and unwise temperament. It tells us that, "a fool is cursed" and his heart becomes deceitful above all things (Jeremiah 17:5-9). The prophet declared that "those who forsake the Lord will be ashamed in the day of reckoning". The lack of self-respect made the Israelites spies feel unworthy of their inheritance. There is a very distinguished commentary that says, "He who separates himself seeks his own desire, he quarrels against all sound wisdom" (Proverbs 18:1 NASB).

The Bible says, *"The fear of the Lord is the beginning of knowledge. Fools despise wisdom and instruction"* (Proverbs 1:7 NIV). The absence of spiritual wisdom can lead to a lack of ability to function proficiently in the things of God. This can be compared to the academically qualified person who compares their wisdom to someone unqualified in their eyes. It is more difficult to accept wisdom from someone they presume is underqualified. However, the spiritual intellectual person is defined as one that demonstrates the wisdom of God. Today, it is not a popular subject to discuss the manifestations of having spiritual wisdom and discernment. On this topic, the Bible mentions that the kings and prophets functioned in the wisdom of God. Nevertheless, there is mention of those kings and prophets who led the people in rebellion against the Lord, and this was distinguished as "evil in the sight of God."

There are some people that would display foolishness and they require a reflection of godly character. People in different walks of life need the wisdom of God to interact with those that walk in ungodly wisdom. This is even found in the church today, Jesus even mentioned this in His messages. James encourages an individual to conduct themselves wisely in wisdom and understanding with some measure of discernment. The Bible tells us, "The quiet words of the wise are more to be heeded than the shouts of a ruler of fools. Wisdom is better than weapons of war, but one sinner destroys much good" (Ecclesiastes 9:18 NIV).

Moreover, the book of Proverbs describes a distinction between a wise woman and a foolish woman. It states, *"The wise woman builds her house, but the foolish woman pulls it down with her hands"* (Proverbs 14:1 NKJV). The explanation I found for this verse states that a foolish woman pulls down the foundation of her house by adopting destructive habits that can be spiteful and careless to cause poverty to her family. The topic of the wise woman is also discussed in a later chapter.

The Bible admonishes you as a believer of Jesus Christ never to put your trust in man's wisdom or in their enticing words. It encourages you to trust in God and in His power of the demonstration of His Spirit. In other words, a believer should not let their faith stand in the wisdom of men, but in the power of God. Apostle Paul states, *"God has commanded light to shine out of darkness, who has shone in our hearts to give the light of the knowledge of the glory of God in face of Jesus Christ"* (2 Corinthians 4:6-7 NKJV).

The Bible says that Abigail rode her donkey and advanced towards the hills where David and his men were with gifts of provision. She dismounted and fell at David's feet in reverence. Then in her humility, she pleaded for forgiveness, confessed that her husband was foolish; and asked David to put Nabal's iniquity upon her instead. Maybe Abigail was familiar with the meaning of her husband's name, for the Hebrew word for "Nabal" means "a fool" or "foolish." The Bible recognizes her as a wise woman who understood the hand of God was upon David's life. At the end of the story, her husband Nabal died and was taken out of the picture

THE DISTINCTION OF THE IMPRUDENT

by God himself. After his death, David was told the news and he sent for Abigail to become his wife (I Samuel 25).

The person of wisdom asked a question to Hosea to predetermine a prophecy to the children of Israel. The statement concluded that the Lord wished to see those who would trust Him in the full manifestation of His wisdom and continue in the path of righteousness. The scripture contrast two paths – the way of the righteous and the ungodly way. However, the prophet Hosea declared, "For the ways of the Lord are right, and the just shall walk in them" (Hosea 14:9 KJV).

One of the crucial causes of spiritual blindness is the inability to see the truth. This skepticism is often compared to the blindness that is likened to a fool. Jesus was able to discern by the gift of revelation. He referred to the character of a fool when He asked the following questions, "Can the blind lead the blind? Will they not both fall into a pit?" (Luke 6:39 NIV). In other words, "Can a fool lead a fool?"

I heard a Bible scholar once say that ungodly wisdom is anything that disconnects us from God. It is an abomination, and therefore, to ignore God's will is ultimately a form of idolatry. The scripture makes this clear to the believer saying, "Those that lack wisdom and knowledge did not choose the fear of the Lord." Without choosing to honor the Lord our God, the word of knowledge and understanding, which are gifts from God will not flow freely. My prayer is for you to choose Christ Jesus as your Savior and receive the inheritance of the gift of wisdom and understanding.

The Sages suggest that as a man or woman walks with God, he or she should manifest godly wisdom, joy, hope, peace, and other attributes of God which are limited to godly counsel.

The Contradictory Wisdom

The story of Job, in essence, reveals Job's reaction to his trials that resulted in heartache. He became irrational or unwise in his thoughts and his speech (Job 34:35). Job was knowledgeable of God, and yet his instinct betrayed him to believing that his circumstance was a chastening from the hand of God. His wisdom said that he could still hear the voice of God when the Lord answered Job out of a whirlwind and said, *"Who is this that obscures my plans with words without knowledge?"* (Job 38:2 NIV). God spoke to Job and asked his reason for speaking foolishly, for there is a similarity to the language of the unwise. Job was persuaded to confess his shame.

Another prophet, whose name was Jonah was a prime challenger of God's wisdom. He acted irrational when he received the instruction from the Lord to go to the city of Nineveh with a prophecy of judgment. In Jewish history, they say that Nineveh was part of Assyria, and the Assyrians were involved in idolatry and the captivity of the children of Israel in the time of King Hezekiah (Isaiah 36:1 KJV). In those days many people were involved in committing abominations against God. The Prophet was instructed by God to go and reveal the future of Nineveh. It was during this time that God was ready to judge Nineveh. Therefore, He sent Jonah to warn them that their judgment was at hand and their chance to repent was now.

Jonah was aware of Nineveh's atrocities against the Jews, and he preferred God to totally judge the people without mercy. This was the reason Jonah chose to be disobedient to the Lord. His unwise actions landed him in his own dilemma. The Bible tells us that Jonah was casted out of a boat and he endured the belly of a whale for three days and nights. God made the whale regurgitate Jonah on the shore of the vicinity of Nineveh on the third day. This revelation of God's plan was executed, and Jonah delivered the warning to the city of Nineveh. The people of Nineveh received Jonah's warnings, and the scripture says that immediately they called a fast to refrain from their sins. Their humility and repentance turned the mind of God from judgment. The Bible declares, *"The Lord is slow to anger but great in power; the Lord will not leave the guilty unpunished"* (Nahum 1:3 NIV). In this scenario, Jonah acknowledged, *"When God saw their deeds, that they turned from their evil way, then God relented of the disaster which He had declared He would bring on*

THE DISTINCTION OF THE IMPRUDENT

them. So, He did not do it" (Jonah 3:10 NASB). Jesus mentioned the repentance of the men of Nineveh in His teachings. Their repentance was revered by God and they were genuine in their turning back to God.

The apostle Paul admonished the believers that in the future days, the Lord will judge the secrets of men. He suggested that they would not be found innocent. In those days, many of the leaders were boastful of their Jewish laws and yet they used their understanding unwisely. Paul recognized that that character of these Jewish leaders' was of an outward appearance, but their hearts were sinful (Roman 2:16-29). Paul asserted that the laws were to be a guide to the blind, and a light to them which are in darkness or unwise. The leaders were supposed to be teachers of the unlearned in Christ, but they walked in only a form of knowledge and truth of God's law that they preached. For example, a man should not steal. They were hypocrites and they dishonored God by breaking His laws themselves. The apostle Paul likened their action to that of a fool. This sounds very familiar in the body of Christ today.

The apostle Paul taught the believers the fundamental way to walk with the Lord Jesus Christ. He says that it is a faith walk and not about your works. The believer is required to be in a right relationship with God and he correctly implied that we are to be separated from the norm to live in the righteousness of God. He mainly focused on the moral stance pertaining to our personal righteousness.

There is no suggestion found in the scriptures that King Solomon was not knowledgeable of Jewish cultural morals. According to the Bible, King Solomon had a heart of wisdom to counsel in justice, which was better than any other king in all their days. His distinction was known in all the nations as he also possessed much wealth. However, Solomon's foolish acts of sin displayed his rejection of the covenant with the Lord. His actions produced the dimness of his spiritual light as a wise man when he married wives of other nations against God's commands. The Sages say that Solomon may have expected that this unwise decision would create alliances among nations.

King Solomon revealed in his writings the many failures of his life that entailed spiritual and natural wisdom. His wisdom was greatly influential in the dating arena, and it became perverted to an ungodly wisdom which resulted in the judgment of God. Solomon eventually lost the kingdom and later he acknowledged his mistakes. He used his experience to caution the people in his declaration to say, *"Folly is joy to him that is destitute of wisdom: but a man of understanding walketh uprightly"* (Proverbs 15:21 KJV). In another translation it says, *"Foolishness is joy to one who lacks sense, but a person of understanding walks straight"* (NASB). *"A fool is a person void of godly wisdom and their act of foolishness is the denial of the Truth of God."* One of the Hebrew commentaries stated that Solomon's foolishness made Israel temporarily bankrupt spiritually and physically for several years.

The Bible explicitly separated the wisdom of Abigail and her husband Nabal. A Hebrew commentary suggests that Nabal was foolish in his response to David in the time of his distress. In the story, David fled the city from Saul, they came into the district and heard of the recognition of Nabal. Therefore, David sent ten of his men to ask bread and meat of Nabal. He refused to grant David's request and it portrayed him as an inconsiderate person towards the men of Israel. This could have cost him his life. The Bible tells us that on receiving the report from his men, David became angry, he armed his men to journey to do Nabal and his household harm. Fortunately, one of his servants told Abigail what transpired and how David and his men had not been a bother to them while they were in the field with the cattle. Therefore, Nabal's servants felt more secure with their presence in the wilderness.

Now the reaction of Abigail was different from her husband's. In her wisdom, she gathered supplies and loaded the donkeys. She journeyed in the direction in which she knew the men were advancing towards her home. She was aware of David's bravery and all his achievements of victory in many wars for Israel during those days. Therefore, when she met David on their path, she displayed

THE DISTINCTION OF THE IMPRUDENT

humility and respect for his might. She purposed in her heart to do something to save her household from destruction at the hand of David. She knew that Nabal's servants were innocent. In her wisdom, she never mentioned her intentions to her husband.

> *"Curse be the man that trusteth in man, and maketh flesh his arm, and whose heart departeth from the Lord."*
> (Jeremiah 17:5 KJV)

Chapter 14

The Peculiarity of the Wise

The Bible clarifies that there is a variance between a wise man and a foolish man. This phrase from a Godly perspective shows that a fool denies truth and is without the wisdom of God. To reiterate the character of a fool, it is simply described as one that is unaware of God's word by faith. The scripture says, "The fool has said in his heart, there is no God" (Psalm 14:1 KJV).

In scripture it says, "Do not forsake wisdom, and she will protect you; love her, and she will watch over you" (Proverbs 4: 6-7 NIV). In other words, wisdom expects you to love her. There is another scripture that says, "The path of life leads upward for the wise to keep him from going down to the grave (NIV). I found this very intriguing that the scripture says, "Wisdom is a defense as money is a defense. But the excellence of knowledge is that wisdom gives life to those who have it" (Ecclesiastes 7:12 NIV). The Bible also tells us that "Through desire a man, having separated himself, seeketh and intermeddleth with all wisdom" (Proverbs 18:1 KJV). Evidently, there is a distinction between a wise and an unwise person. This reveals that the natural wisdom of a man is associated with foolishness towards God (1 Corinthians 3:19).

According to Apostle Paul, the foolishness of God is even wiser than men's wisdom (1 Corinthians 1:25). The word of God defined such wisdom by the message of the cross. It states that people who are unwise have an issue with comprehending the truth that Christ Jesus hung on a cross to save the souls of men. He gave salvation and sanctification to the believer by faith.

"Get wisdom, get understanding: forget it not; neither decline from the words of my mouth. Forsake her not, and she shall preserve thee: love her, and she will keep thee."
(Proverbs 4: 5-6 KJV)

As Jesus taught the people, He used the Beatitudes to imply that the wise in spirit are blessed. These statements were like resonance of the Commandments that God gave to Moses so that the people may be directed in righteous living. He explained that the wise in spirit will inherit the earth. In other words, the meek and humble will inherit the earth. The Psalmist says, "The Lord guides the humble in what is right and teaches them his way" (Psalm 25:9 NIV). In this analogy, Jesus compared the characteristics of the believer and what they needed to possess, to that of a foolish person.

On a particular Mount, Jesus' "Beatitude" sermon offered a pathway of life which is comprised of the promise of eternity in His heavenly kingdom (Matthew 5:3-10). According to these scriptures, there is a fundamental of life which has a positive sense of virtue. In one of the verses, Jesus proclaimed to his disciples, "Those who hunger and thirst for righteousness are blessed and they will be satisfied." The Sages say that Jesus encouraged them to unceasingly desire wisdom for justice and moral excellence that would lead to their spiritual fulfillment and their transition to godliness. Another scholar noted that the gift of the spirit of God is necessary to fulfill the Beatitudes. Such godly wisdom is intended to be accessible only in our obedience.

The Eight Beatitudes of Jesus

"Blessed are the poor in spirit
for theirs is the kingdom of heaven.

Blessed are those who mourn,
for they will be comforted.

Blessed are the meek,
for they will inherit the earth.

Blessed are those who hunger and thirst for righteousness,
for they will be satisfied.

THE PECULIARITY OF THE WISE

Blessed are the merciful,
for they will be shown mercy.

Blessed are the pure in heart,
for they will see God.

Blessed are the peacemakers,
for they will be called children of God.

Blessed are those who are persecuted because of righteousness,
for theirs is the kingdom of heaven."
(Matthew 5:3-10 NIV)

The psalmist David compared the righteous man to a wise person and as one full of the spirit of wisdom. He declared that their righteousness is wise and of a gracious and giving personality. David proclaimed, *"The steps of a good man are ordered by the Lord: and he delighteth in his way"* (Psalm 37:23 KJV). Interestingly, there was a Jewish commentary that described this verse as "a righteous man hates falsehood." They say that a righteous man watches his words and speaks carefully. This idiom is very applicable to all the fake news that is heard today.

We read in the book of Proverbs, *"The mouth of the righteous is a fountain of Life"* (Proverbs 10:11). This phrase can be interpreted as *"wise counsel comes from within the heart of the righteous."* This is very revealing, according to the Bible, *"The fruit of the righteous is a tree of life, and the one who is wise saves lives"* (Proverbs 11:30 NIV).

The word of God encourages us to pursue wisdom and understanding in all our desires. The scripture admonishes us that "the people of God perish because of a lack of knowledge" (Hosea 4:6). In this case, there is a distinction of those who lack knowledge that can relate to the need of something. One definition says the word "lack" means, "There is not sufficient knowledge, information, or training about something." This word "lack" could be interpreted as "the reason for being uninstructed, untrained, or uneducated in a particular matter." This is basically "unexperienced or unaware."

Throughout the Bible, wisdom is exemplified of the wise person that would hear and increase their knowledge through the counsel of the Holy Spirit (Proverbs 1:5). The gift of the Holy Spirit is for the edifying of the saints (1 Corinthians 12:4-10). Therefore, if we lack wisdom, we must cultivate a desire for the gift of God (which is a diversity of gifts) to walk in wisdom, discernment, counsel, healing, and to be filled with the Holy Ghost.

The Advantages of Wisdom

"Let him who glorifies, glory in this, that he understands and knows me, that I am the Lord exercising loving-kindness, judgement, and righteousness, in the earth. For in these I delight, says the Lord."
(Jeremiah 9:24 NKJV)

The word of God is a valuable tool and guide to light that reveals the truth of successful living. The Bible is a source of the principles of righteousness for the worth of wisdom, the propagation of righteous justice, and for success and good health. It includes evidence and insight of the life of God, His creation, and His plan for humanity. The information that is revealed by reading and understanding the precepts of God's wisdom is attained through the Holy Spirit.

The Bible tells us that Jesus said to His disciples, "Truly, truly, I say to you, the one who hears My word, and believes Him who sent Me, has eternal life, and does not come into judgment, but has passed out of death into life" (John 5:24 NASB). John indicated that Jesus told the disciples to willingly hear and believe His words and, they will have the benefit of everlasting life. In this statement, Jesus showed that there was no room for doubt. He concluded to those who believed that He was sent from God that they will never

THE PECULIARITY OF THE WISE

be condemned for their sins, but they are forgiven and have passed from the judgment of death to eternal life with YHVH (God). It was the testimony of John that declared, "God so loved the world that He gave His only Son, so that everyone who believes in Him (Yeshua) will not perish but have eternal life" (John 3:16 NASB).

The almond tree is a fascinating plant. They are known to quickly produce fruit in its season. It is said that it brings forth flowers and leaves in twenty-one days as the fruit is hastily ripened. The almond branch is the representation of Israel according to Hebraic tradition. The Lord used this revelation of the almond tree and gave the prophet Jeremiah a vision of the twig of the almond branch. Jeremiah was called to attention and God interpreted the vision telling him that this was a symbol of the swift fulfilment of His word concerning Israel. Jeremiah's response was to prophesy the fulfillment of judgment of the children of Israel in crisis in his day.

Afterwards, Jeremiah proclaimed to the people of Israel, "God watches over His word to perform it" (Jeremiah 1:12).

The wisdom of a man is referenced in the book of Proverbs as the one who keeps the word of God and the laws of His commands (Proverbs 28:7). The advantage of spiritual wisdom is to understand the word of God. There is a phrase in the Bible that states the wisdom of a wise man or woman is that they walk in integrity and their children will walk in their blessing after them (Proverbs 20:7). Therefore, the truth of the benefit of wisdom is vital. The Bible tells us, to get wisdom first and then, get understanding. Solomon said that "wisdom must be exalted." This means that "the wisdom of God must be honored." He also stated that "wisdom is the principal thing." Hence, we should get wisdom and understanding.

"Exalt her (Wisdom), and she will promote you; she will bring you honor, when you embrace her. She will place on your head an ornament of grace. A crown of glory she will deliver to you."
(Proverbs 4:5-9 NKJV)

UNDENIABLE WISDOM

These phrases are a testament of the comfort and joy of a wise person who understands the Lord is our defense (Psalm 5:11-12). In Solomon's wisdom, he stated the advantage of having spiritual wisdom. The scripture says, *"Forget it not; neither decline from the words of my mouth. Forsake her not, and she shall preserve thee: love her, and she shall keep you"* (Proverbs 4:5-6 KJV). Wisdom is supreme, therefore, get wisdom. Though it costs all you have, get understanding (Proverbs 4:6-7). This phrase was very explicit to the need for wisdom which shows that a life without the wisdom of God may well be characterized as a life of dishonor, regret, and misery.

With an authoritative impact, the ministry of Jesus shows that there was a presence of the divine wisdom. On some occasions, Jesus taught that He only did what His heavenly father told Him to do. Jesus' teaching to his disciples said, *"All things are delivered unto me of my Father: and no man knoweth the Son, but the Father; neither knoweth any man the Father, save the Son, and he to whomsoever the son will reveal him"* (Matt 11:29 KJV). Moreover, the Bible reveals that Jesus Christ is good. He healed those that were sick and delivered those who were oppressed of the devil.

The apostle Paul addressed the wisdom of God in the name of Jesus Christ. He revealed that the gift of God was inclusive of the wisdom of God. Such wisdom is the understanding of the Passover, redemption and sanctification. What God did by sending His son Yeshua, to die on the cross was of divine wisdom. Paul said this to encourage the believer to have a yearning for the gifts of God. He made the declaration that "wisdom is divine and profitable." He alluded to Jesus Christ as the foundation of divine wisdom.

We can read of the wisdom of Moses, Samuel, Samson, and many other prophets of the Bible. King David cultivated a repentant heart towards the Lord, as he prayed with remorse for his sins. The promises of God, with his faith, over time developed David's trust in God gave him an advantage to endure many trails in his life. David was a prime example of a humble and a contrite heart. He immersed himself in the word of God and the prophets. David's

THE PECULIARITY OF THE WISE

reaction to these times made him declare that "God is the only true and wise God." He genuinely repented and the Lord blessed him with the spirit of wisdom. In his days, David was a discerner of God's mercy and grace. Subsequently, the Bible tells us that the Lord forgave David of all his iniquities and sins and called him His friend. The king declared that the Laws of God are perfect and that they convert the soul. The testimony of the Lord is sure (Psalm 19:7). Even today, people benefit from rehearsing David's prayers, as his worship is famous to exalting God. In one of his writings, the psalmist proclaimed, *"How can a young man cleanse his way? By taking heed according to your word"* (Psalm 119:9 NKJV).

The prophet Daniel declared, *"The people that do know their God will be strong and do exploits"* (Daniel 11:32 KJV). God wants to give us wisdom and knowledge of Him so that His extraordinary nature and power can do mighty deeds that would reveal the witness of the reality of who Jesus is to us. In the New Testament, the Lord Jesus Christ gave his disciples the key to operate in wisdom and discernment. Jesus said unto Peter, "I will give you the keys of the kingdom of heaven; whatever you bind on earth will be bound in heaven, and whatever you loose on earth will be loosed in heaven" (Matthew 16:19 NIV).

The scripture is profound that says, *"Great is the company of those that published or proclaimed the word of God"* (Psalm 68:11). The apostle Paul declared, *"All scripture is given by inspiration of God, and is profitable for doctrine, for reproof, for correction, for instruction in righteousness"* (2 Timothy 3:16 KJV). This means that the word of God is the wisdom that benefits the believer to right living.

The word of God is His statutes and judgments that are pertinent to life. Therefore, King Solomon penned a scripture which says, *"Trust in the Lord with all your heart, and lean not on your own understanding, in all your ways submit to him, and He will make your paths straight"* (Proverbs 3:5-6 NIV). This phrase indicates that a halfhearted person cannot benefit from all the wisdom of God that He would bestow upon mankind. In the Apostle Paul's writings, he stated that the depth of the riches of wisdom and knowledge are unsearchable, and that God's ways are past finding out (Roman 11:33-36). In other words, Paul defined wisdom as supernatural therefore, none can explain this except the spirit of God. The question was asked by the prophet Hosea, *"Who is wise, and he shall understand these things? prudent, and he shall know them? for the ways of the Lord are right, and the just shall walk in them"* (Hosea 14:9 KJV). Moreover, the spirit of wisdom and discernment is for those who seek after the Lord and turn their ways to his statutes. One of the main ingredients to achieve the wisdom of God is to adhere to His word by receiving and believing God is truth.

Paul, the apostle, admonishes believers to grow up in all things by the word of God. He specified that wisdom and knowledge are indispensable to the reading of God's word (Ephesians 4:14-15). Paul prayed for believers that they would grow in the knowledge of the Lord Jesus Christ (Philippians 3:8). With such knowledge it makes the believer resilient spiritually and gives them an advantage in their livelihood. I read a commentary that says the work of empowerment and intervention of wisdom was only originated from God as the Bible refers to wisdom as the good path.

> *"If you receive my words and treasure my commands within you, so that you incline your ears to wisdom, and apply your heart to understanding; yes, if you cry out for discernment, and lift your voice for understanding, if you seek her as silver, and search for her as for hidden treasures; then you will understand the fear of the Lord, and find knowledge of God. For the Lord give wisdom; from His mouth come knowledge and understanding; He stores up sound wisdom for the upright; He is a shield to those who walk uprightly; He guards the paths of justice, and preserves the way of His saints. Then you will understand righteousness and justice, equity and every good path."*
> (Proverbs 2:1-9 NKJV)

Chapter 15
The Access to Wisdom

"If any of you lacks wisdom, you should ask God."
(James 1:5 NIV)

In the book of James, he declares, *"If any of you lacks wisdom, you should ask God, who gives generously to all, without finding fault, and it will be given to you"* (James 1:5 NIV). This verse reveals that God will freely give the gift of the spirit without reproach. Thus, anyone can ask Him without doubting, and God will give godly wisdom and understanding to those who desire. It can also be said that wisdom from God is an inheritance for the preservation of all believers. The access to wisdom and creativity is wrapped up in the state of every nation with the heart of its people towards God.

The spirit of wisdom has authenticity. It impacted the writer of proverbs to declare, *"I walk in the way of righteousness, along the paths of justice, bestowing a right inheritance on those who love me and making their treasuries full"* (Proverbs 8:20-21 NIV). According to the book of Revelation, the scripture says, "The nations who are saved, they shall walk in the light (of the glory of God), and the kings of the earth will bring their glory and honor into it" (Revelation 21:24).

John the revelator described an incredible occasion. He stated that the people who walk in faithfulness towards God would have access to the New Jerusalem. They will enjoy unique days of the glory of the Lord. The prophet Zachariah foretold, *"On that day the sources of light will no longer shine, yet there will be continuous day! Only the Lord knows how this could happen. There will be no normal day and night, for the evening time it will still be light"* (Zachariah 14:7 NLT). Abraham sought for the heavenly city that is described in the book of Hebrews as a city whose designer and builder is God (Hebrews 11:10-16). This description of the place Abraham pursued was enlightening. He desired God's wisdom in all his affairs to expedite His glory. The Bible tells us that the saved rulers of the earth will enjoy access to that heavenly city and will bring their glory into it. Therefore, God's glory and wisdom must be included in all our affairs.

The prophet Joel assured the people that God will cause an outpouring of the supernatural blessing of wisdom and revelations in the last days. The present-day signs are already in support of this, and the people of God are experiencing such revelations of prophecy. The prophet declared thus said the Lord, *"It shall come to pass afterward that I will pour out my spirit on all flesh"* (Joel 2:28 NKJV), and *"I will show wonders in the heavens and in the earth, blood and fire and pillars of smoke"* (Joel 2:30 NKJV).

Even the signs in the heavens are revealing the preparation of the coming of the Lord our Savior. The signs of the moon are causing scientists to be baffled; they cannot determine these signs in the skies. Recently, there were many unpredictable widespread fires and strange occurrences that are happening on the earth.

God's desire is to bless us with knowledge and understanding of the times that we live in. However, many people are limited in their access to godly wisdom today; this can be determined by our desire to seek for God's wisdom. There will be no access to divine answers unless the Lord reveals it through the Holy Spirit. In some of Apostle Paul's messages he had spoken of strange events that will transpire before time. He concluded in the verse, *"Eye has not seen, nor ear heard, nor have entered into the heart of man, the things which God has prepared for those who love Him. But God has revealed them to us through His spirit. For the spirit searches all things, yes, the deep things of God"* (1 Corinthians 2:9-10 NKJV).

When Jesus came on the scene everyone was surprised that this could be their Messiah. Their hopes were deterred as their anticipation was just in the form of a humble man. Jesus confounded their human wisdom, and in many cases, they were not able to comprehend what he was teaching. This included the disciples, for Jesus took them aside to give them spiritual revelation.

THE ACCESS TO WISDOM

Paul emphasized that the rulers of that time were not capable of understanding the wisdom of God. He mentioned that they had no knowledge, and they killed the "Lord of Glory."

It is God's spirit who has the capability to reveal the truth about God. The day of Pentecost was a revelation of the access to God's wisdom. The Bible tells us that when the presence of the Lord appeared, they were all filled with the Holy Spirit, and they received access to the mind of Christ (Acts 2).

King Solomon discerned the revelation of the personality of "wisdom" and he proclaimed, *"All the words of my mouth are in righteousness; there is nothing forward or perverse in them"* (Proverbs 8:8-9 KJV). He believed the wisdom of the Lord was the only source of truth, and he compared his thinking completely to an upright living that cannot be observed without divine wisdom. The king David had experienced God and he also declared that the access to wisdom was by way of the word of God. *"The entrance of your words gives light; it gives understanding to the simple"* (Psalm 119:130). In other words, "God's word is enlightening and edifying to the humble." David understood that meditating on the words of God benefitted his thinking and attitude towards truth.

The gospel of Jesus Christ is the recommendation of the "hidden wisdom of God." Paul declared, *"And my speech and preaching were not persuasive words of human wisdom, but in demonstration of the Spirit and of power, that your faith should not be in the wisdom of men but in the power of God"* (1 Corinthians 2:4). The principles of God are written to encourage the believer to understand the effectiveness of obtaining the inconceivable spirit of wisdom.

These keys are basically insights to wisdom.

- *To keep the Word of God; for it is a source of light and life* (Proverbs 7:1-3). This means that the word of God is like an operational manual for living life, and therefore, without this manual we would be ignorant to how it works and how to perceive the light pertaining to the things of God in this dark

world.
- *The word of God is sanctified; and the word is Truth* (John 17:17). The Bible says that the word of God is consecrated and holy for only truth is found therein. God is truth; therefore, He cannot lie.
- *The word is Spirit and the Spirit gives life* (John 6:63). Jesus said, "The words he spoke were full of the Spirit and life. God is the manifestation of the essence of His word and He is the foundation of life.
- *The word of God will make you become wiser and brighter* (Proverb 4:18). The written word of God is the wisdom and brightness of the illumination of His holy presence.
- *The knowledge of God is a necessity* (Deuteronomy 28). The Lord promised the children of Israel that if they served Him; then, none of the diseases shall come upon them that came upon the Egyptians.
- *God's counsel is faithfulness and Truth* (Isaiah 25:1). "O Lord, you are my God, I will exalt you; I will praise your name, for you have done wonderful things." The prophet Isaiah noted that God was faithful in all He has done concerning Israel. The revelation knowledge we learn is that God is truth. This highlights that in the heaven there is a language of truth and there is no place for untruth.

Another scripture tells us that wisdom *"shall be health to your navel, and marrow to thy bones"* (Proverbs 3:7-8 KJV). This phrase is an awesome illustration of a Hebrew scholar analyzing the wisdom of the man or woman. The writer compared wisdom to the food given to a newborn child. He stated that the scriptures are likened to the natural guarantee that an infant should be fed spiritually as well as naturally for their growth and development.

King Solomon gave a prophecy of wisdom. He declared,

THE ACCESS TO WISDOM

"Attend to my words; incline your ear unto my sayings. Do not let them depart from your eyes; keep them in the midst of your heart; for they are life to those who find them, and health to all their flesh. Keep your heart with all diligence, for out of it springs the issues of life" (Proverbs 4:20-23 NKJV). He suggested that to achieve wisdom was to be attentive to every word that comes from the breath of God. He states the action of inclining one's ear to listen attentively and receptively to what God is saying is wisdom. This phrase was used very often in the Bible to bring attention to the hearer. "I have called upon You, for You will hear me, O God; Incline Your ear to me, and hear my speech" (Psalm 17:6).

God was requesting His people to love His wisdom and to keep it close to their hearts. He wants them to teach their future generations the love of God and how He delivered them from all their enemies. God commanded Moses to speak to the children of Israel saying:

"Hear, O Israel: The Lord our God is one Lord:
And thou shalt love the Lord thy God with all thine heart,
and with all thy soul, and with all thy might.
And these words, which I command thee this day,
shall be in thine heart.
And thou shall teach them diligently unto thy children,
and shalt talk of them when thou sittest in thine house,
and when thou walkest by the way, and when thou liest
down, and when thou risest up.
And thou shalt bind them for a sign upon thine hand,
and they shall be as frontlets between thine eyes.
And thou shalt write them upon the posts of thy house,
and on thy gates"
(Deuteronomy 6:4-6 KJV).

These scriptures reveal that God's heart yearns for a relationship with mankind. He wants us to seek His face for the help we need. Knowing that God loves us should propel our self-confidence to desire the wisdom and knowledge of God. To bring about a wholehearted success, the wisdom that is required cannot only be of a natural knowledge, but a spiritual wisdom that is divine that the prophet talked about, that dwells on the inside of mankind.

A Place of Wisdom

In the place of godly wisdom, the Bible teaches that it has correlation to the condition of the heart. King David, by faith, prayed and asked the Lord to change his heart. His desire for wisdom related to his faith in the provision of God. Another Bible story that required a place of wisdom was in the plight of Joseph when he encountered Potiphar's wife. He was steadfast in his belief and his characteristics of holiness determined his declaration for truth, *"How can I do this thing against my God."* In this situation, Joseph's heart was sold out to the Lord, he was on a one-way street to his redemption. His thoughts of compromising his belief were untainted. He understood wisdom and discernment from the biblical point of view.

The Bible says, "God is no respecter of persons." This scripture can be revised as, "God is Wisdom" or "Wisdom is no respecter of persons." This scripture refers to wisdom as a feminine character who speaks in every tongue, to every people. I submit that wisdom is talkative, and this is very familiar to godly characters. The Sages believe that there is some amount of wisdom to be found in each person at birth. The scripture tells us that the Lord in His wisdom gave each of His creation an individual manifestation of the knowledge of God the Father. Hence, the prospective of every man's heart is designed with a customized spiritual wisdom.

The Bible emphasizes what is true wisdom and understanding:

1. *"Wisdom rests in the heart of him who has understanding"* (Proverbs 14:33 NKJV). This means that wisdom is found on the inside of a man's heart and spirit. Our souls need to correlate

to our spiritual mind.
2. *When wisdom enters your heart, and knowledge is pleasant to your soul"* (Proverbs 2:10). Another translation says, "For wisdom will enter your heart, and knowledge will be pleasant to your soul" (NIV).

   "A wise man will hear, and will increase learning; and a man of understanding shall attain unto wise counsels" (Proverbs 1:5). The word for *"hear"* means "to hear the word of God is a skill of learning that leads to understanding and would give wise counsel."
3. *"According to the revelation of the mystery, kept secret since the world began, but now made manifest, and by the prophetic scriptures made known to all nations, according to the commandment of the everlasting God, for obedience to the faith"* (Romans 16:25-26 NKJV). The apostle Paul was teaching of the wisdom that can only be acquired by the leading of the Holy Spirit.
4. *He reveals the deep and secret things; He knows what is in the darkness, and the light dwells with him* (Daniel 2:2). The prophet Daniel acknowledged that only God could reveal the things that are hidden from the natural eyes.
5. *Surely the Lord God does nothing, unless He reveals His secret to His servants the prophets* (Amos 3:7). Amos recognized that he had to depend on God to tell the things of judgment and justice in the future.

The psalmist David says, *"The steps of a good man are ordered by the Lord, and he delights in his ways"* (Psalm 37:23 NKJV). The scripture also says, *"Who is the man that fears the Lord? Him shall He teach in the way He chooses"* (Psalms 25:12 NKJV). This scripture encourages us to access spiritual wisdom which will guide our way. "There in God are hidden all the treasures of wisdom and knowledge," according to the apostle Paul. In one of his prayers for the Laodicean people, Paul prayed that "their hearts might be comforted in their togetherness in love. That all the riches of the full assurance of understanding, the acknowledgment of the mystery of God, the Father, and of Christ be revealed" (Colossians 2:2-3). Paul also acknowledged the Bereans who were probably Gentiles, sought after the wisdom of the word of God day after day to ensure that Paul and Silas were teaching the truth (Acts 17:11).

"This is the confidence that we have in Him, that if we ask anything according to His will, He hears us. And if we know that He hears us, whatever we ask, we know that we have the petitions that we have asked of Him."
(1 John 5:140-15 NKJV)

As we consider the process of growth and development of a small child in the prospective of wisdom, scientists suggest that the child's mannerisms can be visibly imitated by the godly principle practiced in the home. For instance, in every family there are complements of each individual gift. Seemly, the wisdom of the Lord operates in different dimensions that should amaze parents. Each person displays their point of view of their natural knowledge as they respond to a situation. Then, according to their spiritual wisdom, it will reveal the diverse facets of instinctiveness, creativity, and a level of education. Another facet of wisdom is the capability given to motherhood as well as fatherhood. God has blessed parents with a natural and spiritual counsel ability that is astounding.

In Daniel's days, he prophesied of a time to come. He said, *"Those who are wise shall shine like the brightness of the firmament, and those who turn many to righteousness like the stars for ever and ever, many shall run to and fro, and knowledge shall increase"* (Daniel 12:3-4 NKJV). He tells us that the upright in God, those who are wise would bring the ones who seek God wisdom to the truth with

THE ACCESS TO WISDOM

the help of the Holy Spirit; those shall be wise to win souls for the kingdom of God (Matthew 13:43). The Judge of all the earth will certainly do right; and when he cometh, his reward is with him, to give every man according as his work shall be (Revelation 22:12). Therefore, it is a full assurance that the righteous will be rewarded for their interest in the spiritual and eternal interests of others.

King Solomon recognized that wisdom and favor from God are interrelated. In his declaration he says, *"A good man obtains favor from the Lord"* (Proverbs 12:2 NKJV). In other words, the righteous one can obtain good success in the aspect of wisdom, understanding, and blessing in the sight of God and man.

Today, the place of wisdom is needed as we have need for the Savior. His name is Jesus Christ, the Messiah and King of the universe.

Chapter 16
Wisdom is a Medicine

"A Merry heart does good, like medicine, but a broken spirit dries the bones."
(Proverbs 17:22 NKJV)

Wisdom in the natural world can be defined as a gift from God. However, it has limitations. Godly wisdom is likened to the characteristics of holistic medicine. Today, this phrase seems difficult for many people because of the circumstances of everyday life. When we think of how natural science defines humankind; it suggests that humans are a tripartite being. Their natural components are the soul, the spirit and the body. There are scriptures to back up the applicability of this scientific facts (1 Thessalonians 5:23, Mathew 10:28 and Galatians 5:16-17 NKJV).

The spiritual component of the man is connected to communication with God. The body is the physical nature or fleshly part of the man, and the soul is connected to the heart of a man, his thoughts, and emotions.

In holistic medicine the natural remedy that a physician usually focuses on is the parts that are inclusive of a healthy outcome. They advise their patient to eat wellness foods, exercise and meditate on good thoughts. Similarly, in the spiritual aspect of life, a godly spiritual advisor will recommend the word of God, the Holy Spirit, and a dose of godly wisdom. These main components produce a lifetime of instantaneous results of a healthy lifestyle, good morals, and spiritual benefits beyond the natural wisdom of a man.

In this chapter, the scripture reminds us that wisdom is a product of a merry heart. The dictionary describes a "merry heart" as a heart that is full of cheerfulness and joyous in spirit. It is full of laughter and happiness. The word "merry" can also be translated as "joyful, good and a glad heart." Also, it says that a happy heart is like medicine and it causes the mind to heal. In Proverbs, it declares that "a merry heart is recommendable as medicine." King Solomon made feasts and celebrated the Lord in a way to encourage everyone to be joyful and humor themselves in the process of their lifetime. The psalmist David recognized wisdom from God as pleasurable and satisfying to the soul. He declared, *"How sweet are your words to my taste, sweeter than honey to my mouth!"* (Psalm 119:103 NIV). In another verse David also proclaimed, *"Great peace have those who love your "law" and nothing can make them stumble"* (Psalm 119:165 NIV).

Historic evidence shows that the people traveled and there were none feeble amongst them. The word of God is powerful. Wisdom is in the laws of God (Deuteronomy 4:6). The Bible portrays many incidences where the Jewish people were knowledgeable of the healing power of God. God's word was His bond, and He told Moses He would heal the people. Throughout their journey in the wilderness, the children of Israel experienced healing and deliverance. The scripture says they were in the desert where no water was available, and the Lord miraculously made a stream in the desert to quench their thirst. This supernatural water was like medicine to their thirsty souls.

The Bible also tells us that the manna God sent from heaven was likened to food and medicine to the physical soul. Matthew stated that "healing was the children's bread." Bread in this phrase signifies nourishment for the body. Jesus did offer spiritual bread to his followers to feed their spiritual needs. This was His way of offering a way to salvation. His compassion for humanity is evident, for he again signified the love of God to heal the people. *"I am the bread of life. Whoever comes to me will never be hungry again. Whoever believes in me will never be thirsty"* (John 6:35 NLT) "for the true bread of God is the one who comes down from heaven and gives life to the world" (John 6:33). Moses declared, *"And you shall serve the Lord your God, and He will bless your bread and your water. And I will take sickness away from the midst of you"* (Exodus 23:25 NKJV).

WISDOM IS A MEDICINE

These references in the word of God correlates wisdom likened to medicine.

Wisdom is a healer. Matthew declared that when Jesus walked on the earth, he performed many miracles and healing was one of them. He healed the servant stricken with palsy. He healed blinded eyes, Peter's mother-in-law and all those who were grievously tormented of the devil. According to Matthew, the Lord gave commands to the believers to use wisdom as a medicine to perform miracles. Jesus said, "Heal the sick, cleanse the lepers, raise the dead, cast out devils: freely ye have received, freely give." (Matthew 10:8 KJV).

"God sent his word and healed them; he rescued them from them grave" (Psalm 197:20 NIV). His word is more powerful than any destruction.

"Behold, I will bring it health and cure, and I will cure them, and will reveal unto them the abundance of peace and truth" (Jeremiah 33:6 KJV).

"She is a tree of life" (Proverbs 3:18 NIV).

"For they are life to those who find them, and health to all their flesh" (Proverbs 4:22 NKJV).

"It will be health to your flesh. And strength to your bones" (Proverbs 3:8 NKJV).

"He heals the broken hearted and binds up their wounds" (Psalm 147:3 NIV).

"Pleasant words are as a honeycomb, sweet to the soul, and health to the bones" (Proverbs 16:24 KJV).

UNDENIABLE WISDOM

"Through wisdom your days will be many" (Proverbs 9:11 NIV).

"For length of days and long life and peace they will add to you." (Proverbs 3:2 NKJV).

"The wisdom from above is first pure, then peace-loving, gentle, reasonable, full of mercy and good fruits, impartial, free from hypocrisy" (James 3:17 NASB).

- *Wisdom performs duties.* Wisdom can multitask and there are many dimensions of its character that are revisited.
- *Wisdom is joy and happiness and full of glory.*
- *Wisdom revives.*
- *Wisdom brings peace* (Proverbs 11:12).
- *Wisdom guides.*
- *Wisdom seeks.*
- *Wisdom leads you to repentance;* the Hebrew for repentance is "Teshuvah."
- *Wisdom is wholeness,* it is not partial or fragmented.
- *Wisdom is knowledge and understanding.*
- *Wisdom instructs* (Proverbs 3:29)
- *Wisdom saves* – salvation. "By grace are ye saved through faith; and that not of yourselves: It is the gift of God" (Ephesians 2:8).
- *Wisdom is light.* Jesus said, "I am the light of the world" (John 8:12 NIV). The apostle John declared that Jesus was the light, and in Him was the life, and the life was the light of men." Jesus was declaring that He was the foundation of spiritual light to the world.
- *Wisdom is mercy and truth* (Ps 85:10). The Bible says, "Mercy and truth are met together, righteousness and peace have kissed each other."
- *Wisdom can be inscribed upon the heart.*

WISDOM IS A MEDICINE

The word of Gods says, *"Let not mercy and truth forsake you; bind them around your neck, write them on the tablet of your heart, and so find favor and high esteem in the sight of God and man"* (Proverbs 3:3-4 NKJV). Here is a metaphor of a table on the heart, a revelation of something to consider.

"By wisdom a house is built, and through understanding it is established" (Proverb 24:3 NIV). This reveals the capability of the wholesomeness of wisdom.

An interesting verse of scripture that means "health" says, *"Hope deferred makes the heart sick, but a longing fulfilled is a tree of life"* (Proverb 13:12 NIV). Somehow, this can be interpreted that our unwise desires could cause the heart to be dissatisfied, but the wisdom of God is a source of life and peace.

"And the peace of God, which surpasses all understanding, will guard your hearts and minds through Christ Jesus" (Philippians 4:7 NKJV).

Wisdom dispels darkness (John 1:5). In another verse Jesus said, "I am the light of the world, whoever, follow me will never walk in darkness, but have the light of life." This allegory suggests that the light is the truth, and truth exposes darkness.

Wisdom is a Judge; and does perform justice (Ecclesiastes 3:17). The Bible says that King Solomon prayed to God for an understanding heart to judge the children of God, and to be able to discern between good and evil (1 Kings 3:9). The scripture also mentions that God's divine rebuke is the "rod of His mouth." The "rod" is the correctional tool to express God's Judgment (Isaiah 11:4).

Another verse says, *"Coming out of His mouth is a sharp sword with which to strike down the nations. He will rule them with an iron scepter. He treads the winepress of the fury of the wrath of God Almighty"* (Revelation 19:15 NIV).

Wisdom is the defender of the weak (Psalm 82:3). The Bible tells us that God is that Rock. All His ways are judgment and justice (Deuteronomy 32:4). There is a scripture which says, "The foolishness of God is wiser than men, and the weakness of God is stronger than men (1 Corinthians 1:25).

Wisdom is the bridge between God and man. It refers to the scripture when Jesus said to Thomas, *"I am the way, the truth, and the life. No one comes to the Father except through me"* (John 14:6 NIV). The scripture also says, *"God demonstrates his own love for us in this: while we were still sinners, Christ died for us"* (Romans 5:8 NIV). The idea of wisdom is an advantage to choose the cross to save sinners.

The many sacred keys from the word of God as it applies to our daily walk by faith in Jesus Christ can determine a love relationship with natural and spiritual health. In life a holistic facet of awareness of great information can result in great benefits of health and happiness.

Chapter 17

A Divine Intelligence

There is a story of a divine intelligence that stood out to me in the word of God. It is about a king named Jehoshaphat who reigned over Israel and Judah in his days. The Bible says that all his life he did that which was right in the sight of God, as he sought the Lord for his council. I believe that was by choice.

In instances when his enemies came up against the nation, he cried out to the Lord in his distress. In this predicament King Jehoshaphat received a prophetic word and he trusted God. This story is found in the book of (2 Chronicles 20). The Bible shares that as the people assembled to pray, in their midst the spirit of God came upon Jahaziel, the son of Zechariah; and he prophesied with divine intelligence. Jahaziel proclaimed, *"Thus saith the Lord unto you: Do not be afraid nor dismayed because of this great multitude, for the battle is not yours, but God's"* (2 Chronicles 20:15 NKJV). At that very moment king Jehoshaphat bowed his head with his face to the ground, all the inhabitants of his kingdom fell before the Lord and worshipped Him.

The directions the Lord gave was for them to go out to battle. They took courage to worship and praise God saying, *"Praise the Lord, for his mercy endureth forever"* (2 Chronicles 20:20-21). They had obeyed and believed God that He will fight their enemies. The battle was already victorious as the Lord set ambush against their enemies and they were destroyed. The result of this battle was subjected to multitudes of slain bodies on the ground; none had escaped. Therefore, King Jehosaphat and his people returned to their cities with great spoils. Moreover, on the fourth day of their return, the king made a request for everyone to return to Jerusalem and assemble to the house of the Lord and worshipped with musical instruments. After this incident, the Bible tells us that King Jehoshaphat was at peace with the nations for the remainder of his reign.

UNDENIABLE WISDOM

According to divine wisdom, this supernatural intelligence will lead us to stand still and see the salvation of the Lord. Likewise, divine wisdom will pluck our feet out of every net. Besides, in God's divine intelligence the Lord can produce a criterion of death for his glory. After reading this Bible story, I recognized that there is a supernatural victory against our enemies that will produce a super abundance in our life.

The Omniscient Wisdom

The Bible declares that Jesus functioned as the all-knowing one. There is an illustrated story of the Samaritan woman at Jacob's well. It says that she went there to draw water at the cool of the day and Jesus came to rest at the very hour that she was there. This divine meeting place was the opportunity for the Lord to minister to this woman. According to Jewish history there are historic events that occurred before Jesus came to the earth between the Jews and the Samaritans. This woman had knowledge of the hostility and mistrust that Samaritans had towards Jews and vice versa.

The writer of her story only mentions the dilemma of her past, which had caused her to feel defiled. There was not much detail surrounding this woman, maybe she had been exceptionally beautiful. In her defense, the rumors were factual, for all her relationships were not comfortable with her in the city. Taking these facts into consideration, she would have perceived that Jesus had heard about her through the grapevine. However, as Jesus approached the Samaritan woman, He asked of her a favor first. There was a significant difference in her heart as she stood in his presence. This was unusual to her. Jesus began to compassionately reveal her life events without condemnation. He was aware of her shame and sadness (John 4:16-19). Jesus' approach made her ponder if He was a prophet, and immediately she began to acknowledge her condition. This conversion radically produced a response that divinely restored her confidence, as she recognized that she was in the presence of the Messiah of Israel. That very moment and day, her ministry was launched, and she witnessed to her entire city that she had met the Messiah.

The wisdom of Jesus was insightful. He revealed that at the end of his days there would be fear among his disciples. As they gathered to hear Jesus' teaching, suddenly Peter received a word of knowledge from Jesus. He revealed that Satan desired to sift him as wheat, but Jesus told Peter that He prayed for him, that his faith will not fail (Luke 22:31). Peter overlooked the prophecy that he received and became audacious in his ways as the trial of Jesus Christ progressed. The Bible tells us that on the night of his trial Peter stood close on the porch outside of the court to hear the proceedings. However, a few people who were present on the scene recognized Peter as one of Jesus' disciples. In that moment of their accusation, Peter used profanity and lies to deliver himself out of judgment. Then, he remembered what Jesus said; it was the reality of his situation.

I heard a comment that was truly inspirational to me. It stated, "The devil is very qualified with many degrees; and his degrees are the doctrines of devils." Something to think about.

In one of Jesus' prayers, He asked His father (God) to open the eyes of every believer with wisdom and understanding. He prayed to God that everyone would be empowered to comprehend the spiritual aspect of the kingdom of God and the words of the scriptures. It is something to consider as we desire God's wisdom. Moreover, the psalmist David declares that as you abide in the Lord Jesus Christ, you will receive the revelation of all truth. In a sense, wisdom and understanding are conditional, and there is one place that the divine attribute of wisdom is found.

"He that dwelleth in the secret place of the Most High (God) shall abide under the shadow of the Almighty."
(Psalm 91:1KJV)

UNDENIABLE WISDOM

The Idioms of Solomon

"He stores up sound wisdom for the upright; He is a shield to those who walk uprightly."
(Proverbs 2:7 NKJV)

In my quest for divine wisdom, I began to reflect on the book of Ecclesiastes. The Hebrew Sages stated that the author of the book of Ecclesiastes is unknown. Yet they suggest that the book might have been the writings of King Solomon. As a very famous king his main message was summed up as "fear God and keep His commandments" and "God will bring every deed to judgment." Solomon introduced himself as a preacher, even though he was still subjected to failures. He was obviously still searching for wisdom as he defined his knowledge as a part of his arrogant mistakes. If Solomon was truly the author of this book, he did give mention of his relationship to David as heir to the king of Israel. Solomon's quest for the meaning and purpose of his life apart from God was evident as he left us with a version of the futility of life without placing all our trust in God.

The story tells of Solomon as the young man who God offered anything his heart desired. He gave relation to the seasons and times that speaks to life under the sun. The eloquently detailed factions of his life reflect his kingship and spoke of his love for wealth and greatness. In fact, he had great wealth that surpassed all the kings of his time. Subsequently, Solomon's indulgence in wine and women led him through the dangerous path of foolish decisions.

Here is an insight from Solomon's perspective of the self-importance of knowledge:

"I sought in my heart to give myself unto wine; yet, acquainting mine heart with wisdom; and to lay hold of foolishness, till might see what was that good for the sons of men, which they should do under the heaven. I made me great works, I built me houses; and I planted me vineyards: I made me gardens and orchards, and I planted trees in them of all kind of fruits. I got me pools of water, to water therewith

A DIVINE INTELLIGENCE

the wood that brings forth trees: I got me servants and maidens, and had servants born in my house; also I had great possessions of great and small cattle above all that were in Jerusalem before me: I gathered me also silver and gold, the peculiar treasure of kings and of the provinces: I got me men singers and women singers, and the delights of the sons of men, as musical instruments, and that of all sorts.

Whatsoever, mine eyes desired I kept not from them, I withheld not my heart from my joy; for my heart rejoiced in all my labor: and this was my portion of all my labor. I gave my heart to seek and search out wisdom concerning all things that are done under heaven: this sore travail had God given to the sons of man to be exercised therewith. I communed with my own heart, saying, Lo, I am come to great estate, and have gotten more wisdom than all they that have been before me in Jerusalem: yea, my heart had great experience of wisdom and knowledge. Then I saw that wisdom excels foolishness, as far as light excels darkness. I gave my heart to know wisdom, and to know madness and folly. I dedicated myself to using wisdom for study and discovery of everything under the heaven" (Ecclesiastes 2).

King Solomon likened wisdom from God as the light that excels darkness. Such darkness is related to foolishness. In his early years, he sought the Lord as he desired wisdom and knowledge of the things of God. Solomon could have requested greater things, maybe, as he grew up, he had seen his father seek the Lord before making decisions. David must have played an influential part in Solomon's life; maybe he advised him to ask the Lord for simple things. James admonishes us, that if any lack wisdom, he should ask of God (James 1:5).

God had chosen Solomon to build the temple for the Lord instead of his servant David. This divine wisdom that was placed in Solomon to carry out such a task was a big deal to his father. David must have recognized this assignment from God was not going to be achieved in a natural wisdom alone for his son. The Bible states that David counseled Solomon. Perhaps, Solomon was given the Hebrew traditional books to read the instructions that Noah, Abraham, and Moses received to prepare a place for the almighty God.

Solomon after much delay made the temple for the Lord. Then, he prepared a great feast to honor the Lord. This shows that Solomon was knowledgeable of the things of God. He kept the eight days feast of Rosh Hashanah according to the biblical historians. The story says that even his father, David had accumulated materials to help Solomon to build the tabernacle for the Lord to dwell in.

In one particular scripture Solomon proclaimed, *"He layeth up sound wisdom for the righteous: he is a buckler to them that walk uprightly"* (Proverbs 2:7 KJV). The word "sound" can be interpreted as an "all-compassing range of wisdom to the just," for God is a shield to all of them that is honorable in their walk with the Lord.

Spiritual wisdom is wisdom among those who are mature in faith. It is a mystery of hidden wisdom which is ordained from the God of glory. Paul said if we have great wisdom, they would not have crucified the Lord of Glory. Even today, there are many people who deny wisdom which comes from God. However, this denial is related to the rejecting of the Lord of glory.

Wisdom Entreats of the Mother

"A wise son maketh a glad father,
but a foolish man despiseth his mother."
(Proverbs15:20 KJV)

In the word of God, we read that wisdom implores like a mother to her son. Her great counsel is the skill of humanity. Wisdom in her feminine character is pleasurable to adhere to. Bathsheba was a godly woman and through her experiences as Solomon's mother, she used her wisdom to speak to Solomon about his lifestyle. Her requests made a good functional reference of the plead of all mothers around the world that are serving the Lord Jesus. As follows:

"*My Son! Keep your heart with all diligence, for out of it spring the issues of life*" (Proverbs 4:23 NKJV).

"*Listen, my son, accept what I say, and the years of your life will be many. I instruct you in the way of wisdom and lead you along straight paths"* (Proverbs 4:10-110 NIV).

"My son let not them depart from thine eyes: keep sound wisdom and discretion: so shall they be life unto thy soul, and grace to thy neck" (Proverbs 3:21-22 KJV).

"My son, forget not my law; but let thine heart keep my commandments" (Proverbs 3:1-3 KJV).

"My son, attend to my words; incline thine ear unto my sayings. Let them not depart from thine eyes; keep them in the midst of thine heart" (Proverbs 4:20-22 KJV).

"Only take heed to thyself, and keep thy soul diligently, lest thou forget the things which thine eyes have seen, and lest they depart from thy heart all the days of thy life: but teach them thy sons, and thy sons' sons" (Deuteronomy 4:9 KJV).

Chapter 18
Walking in Divine Wisdom

"The fear of the Lord is the foundation of true wisdom; All Who obey His commands will grow in wisdom."
(Psalm 111:10 NLT)

The Prophet Moses tells us that wisdom is attained by hearing, understanding, and following the precepts of God (Deuteronomy 31:12-13). The word wisdom in the Hebrew language is "chokma." It consists of four letters in their alphabet. According to the Hebrew alphabet each letter has a meaning. The word wisdom occurred over 148 times in the Bible. The Hebrew word "chokma" is associated with the wisdom of ethical and religious affairs, the wisdom of administration; to skill pertaining to war. Being wise is an ability of knowledge and the ability to make right choices.

The scripture tells us that the beginning of true wisdom is established when we fear the Lord (Proverbs 9:10 NKJV). The scholars of the scriptures conclude that walking in the fear or reverence of God will produce great wisdom. The Bible tells us that "Jesus increased in wisdom" (Luke 2:52). This acknowledges that wisdom can actually increase. Moreover, another scripture says that God will give wisdom generously to those that desire wisdom without finding fault. "If any of you lack wisdom, let him ask of God, who giveth to all men liberally, and without reproach, and it will be given to him" (James 1:5). Therefore, everything we need can be obtained through the wisdom of God. We can receive happiness and gain divine understanding to live in financial blessings, and have a long and peaceable life, to live in safety.

A few years ago, I listened to a Hebrew scholar that said divine wisdom is likened to a master key which God has promised to use to preserve our lives in truth forever. In this aspect I would add that wisdom is the primary and highest gift from God. Wisdom is described as more than a good quality; it is absolutely excellent in nature. According to the Oxford dictionary a "quality" is referred to a measured something against other things, or a degree of excellence, standard or value. Hence, divine wisdom can be determined by the value of God's insight that is supernatural, and it would light up your thinking to accomplish a pathway of your divine purpose in the earth.

Therefore, if the Holy Spirit is the custodian of the gift of wisdom, it will produce perfection to our faith. We learn to value these things through divine wisdom and faith. In fact, "wisdom" can be seen as an additional title to the Holy Spirit. King Solomon suggests that we must keep wisdom like an ornament around our neck (Proverbs 1:9). A necklace is a form of ornament worn around the neck to enhance beauty; therefore, wisdom can be affiliated with jewelry to portray grace and beauty. He goes on to say that wisdom will secure our feet from stumbling, and "when thou liest down, thou shalt not be afraid; Yea, thou shalt lie down, and thy sleep shall be sweet" (Proverbs 3:24). In other words, wisdom is responsible for sweet sleep and good security, Amen!

The Holy Spirit or "Wisdom" pleads with all humans to listen to her like sons. God desires for humanity to walk in uprightness and adhere to His commands and statutes. Jesus said, *"I have yet many things to say to you. But you cannot bear them now. When the spirit of truth comes, he will guide you into all truth; for he will not speak on his own authority, but whatever he hears he will speak, and he will declare to you the things that are to come. He will glorify me, for he will take what is mine and declare it to you"* (John 16:12-15).

The Bible admonishes us to believe that all wisdom comes from God. Therefore, we are told to grow in wisdom, in other words "to become wise." Wisdom is an insignia that show the ability to judge correctly as we obey God. It makes us lead effectively in any situation of guidance. King Solomon is known as one of the bible characters who gave great insight to the benefit of wisdom. In the Book of Proverbs, he says, "from His mouth comes knowledge and understanding" (Proverbs 2:6). He is referring to the mouth of the Lord God.

WALKING IN DIVINE WISDOM

In order to receive spiritual wisdom, the Bible declares that we should ask God for it through prayer. God's divine form of wisdom is to act in full compliance to the directive of the Holy Spirit. As a believer, we must understand that the Spirit of God can reveal himself in many facets. These include dreams, visions or through the still small voice, but He is not limited to those facets mentioned alone. God uses His word to reveal Himself to a believer, or he can use another believer to give insight to the things of God. The apostle Paul suggests that the renewing of the mind is essential for spiritual growth.

In the book of Deuteronomy, chapter 4, it can be paraphrased that wisdom from God entails all His words. The bible says, "All Scripture is God-breathed and is useful for teaching, rebuking, correcting, and training in righteousness, so that the servant of God may be thoroughly equipped for every good work" (2 Timothy 3:16-17 NIV). God's secrets can outline the plans He has to establish the abundant life of the believer. God has a glorious plan for each person's life, and in His divine wisdom, He inspires the believer to seek after His will for their lives.

In the book of Isaiah, the prophet reveals that God has already started to make a way. The same can be said of those who trust and believe in His word. In Isaiah, chapter 43, it revealed that the promise of God is to renew the thinking of a people who had experienced hardship, captivity, and problems. According to the prophet, God had intended to redeem and rescue His people. God wanted them to remember what He had done in the past. Yet, He needed them to try to put it behind them, so the new thing could spring forth. Though it seems like a desert place to understand His wisdom, one day He will bring it to pass. God will also change our view spiritually, to discern the things of God in a greater measure. For instance, through the eyes of the spirit, God has revealed the importance of glorifying Him for everything pertaining to life, and to free ourselves from the mindset of our mistakes of the past.

God has the capability in His wisdom to work things out for our good. He desires to use His wisdom to draw us closer to Him.

As a believer, we must trust the Lord to renew our thinking or reasoning concerning the things of God. The question is how can we advance our thoughts into divine wisdom? According to the word of God, the wisdom from above is first pure and authentic. Therefore, God's divine wisdom is needed because our natural wisdom is limited.

There is a scripture that says, *"Oh the depth of the riches and wisdom and knowledge of God! How unsearchable are his judgments and how inscrutable his ways!"* (Romans 11:33). God's wisdom can affect our decisions and even the people around us. It is encouraging to study God's word and to pray for his divine wisdom. We must willingly trust Him.

Your access to wisdom is determined by God, who is divine and can give us access to secret files in His possession. It is very important to seek godly wisdom, it can reveal true happiness, and gives such understanding for good use of life in this society. The benefit of divine wisdom can offer positive and helpful guidance to steer many people away from the wrong direction against the judgment of God.

There are many scriptures in the Bible that give insight on wisdom and knowledge. Also, there are many examples of people who exercised the divine wisdom in all things pertaining to life and godliness. God has bestowed blessings upon those in His economy and He is willing to give divine wisdom to all. Even today, the Lord uses His people to impart wisdom or knowledge to others. In fact, these believers are commended to direct others who need assistance to the things of God through prophecy and word of knowledge.

A fundamental scripture tells us that life is truly spectacular in knowing God and having His wisdom. The scripture verse says, *"Even the youths shall faint and be weary, and the young men shall utterly fall: But they that wait upon the Lord shall renew their strength; they shall mount up with wings as eagles. They shall run, and not be weary; they shall walk, and not faint"* (Isaiah 40:30-31 KJV).

The prophet Isaiah shared that wisdom and the source of our strength is from God. He acknowledges that all mankind gets weary; even our physical strength and abilities are interrelated to the wisdom from God. A wise person needs to depend on the Lord for all guidance and divine wisdom in times of trials or difficult circumstances. The bible tells us, *"Trust in the Lord with all your heart, and do not lean on your own understanding. In all your ways acknowledge him, and he will make straight your paths"* (Proverbs 3:5-6 ESV). *"And we know that all things work together for good to them that love the God, to them who are called according to his purpose"* (Roman 8:28).

This was very enlightening to make mention of in respect to wisdom. In a Hebrew documentary there were explanations of spiritual insight for names and their meaning found in the Bible. The Jewish Sages suggest the importance of the names of their babies. They believe the name of a child plays a significant role in their future. For instance: the name "Joseph" in the Hebrew origin is "He will add." They caution parents to be wise in naming their children.

In my review of wisdom, it has a separate version of wisdom which is defined as a worldly wisdom. This wisdom is exercised without restraints, and it can be said that worldly wisdom has limitation to a godly wisdom. The Bible tells us that the Spirit of God is exceptional to the revealing of the things of God. The natural man does not receive the things of God, for they are foolishness to him. Therefore, he cannot identify or understand spiritual things. However, to signify godly wisdom, it simplifies that a spiritual walk with the Lord governs the divine laws of God. According to the Bible, *"The foolishness of God is wiser than men, and the weakness of God is stronger than men"* (1Corinthians 1:25 ESV).

"Who can know the mind of the Lord that he may instruct Him? But we who have the mind of Christ." Reading the word of God daily is likened to nourishment to your soul and body holistically. The Psalmist declares that *"Your word is light for our path"* (Psalm 119: 105). Light is described as a source of illumination and only God's word has the anointing to give meaning to right and wrong. Therefore, I submit that without the wisdom of God mankind seems to operate out of an alignment with integrity and truthfulness, not being wise. This book has given an extended topic of the undeniable wisdom which can equip one's spiritual development. This truth is the recommendation for a nutritional diet for growth in your faith.

The apostle Peter encouraged the believer to walk in grace and peace, and to multiply in their lives in order not to be stagnant; to grow in the knowledge of Jesus Christ (2 Peter 17-18). He cautioned that without knowledge of God we would become motionless in our wisdom towards the things of God.

My prayer for you today is for the Lord to place a greater measure of divine wisdom and discernment within you. I pray according to Ephesians, chapter 1:17 that "the God of our Lord Jesus Christ, The Father of Glory, may give unto you the spirit of wisdom and revelation in knowledge of him: that the eyes of your understanding being enlightened; that you may know what is the hope of his calling." The Apostle Paul reveals that such wisdom does require a deeper spiritual insight into the secrets of God. My prayer is that your spiritual walk may be victorious in good success, according to the spirit of an overcomer according to (Joshua 1:8). May the purposes of your calling begin to progress in the biblical principles of life and in the light of Jesus Christ.

> *"May the favor of the Lord our God rest on us; establish the work of our hands for us - yes, establish the work of our hands."*
> (Psalm 90:17 NIV)

About the Author

Wynette A Tyrrell is a teacher of the Divine intelligence. Her ministry is dedicated to all ages to enlighten, and to transform by the gospel of Truth. Her writing is a message of the wisdom and power of God.

Her depth of understanding of scripture is reflected in her book. Her writings are an expression of God given wisdom and knowledge which portrays great insight which relates to an intimate relationship with the Holy Spirit.

When you read her books, you are in for a great inspiration and teaching. The thread of excellency flows from one chapter to another with well thought counsel that makes you hunger for more.

Wynette's love and devotion to family is exceptional. She extends her love to the unlovable.

In a sequel to the truth of "Undeniable Wisdom" she has written books entitled, "Look what Jesus did!" and "God's Justice and Judgement."

GOD'S JUSTICE AND JUDGMENT

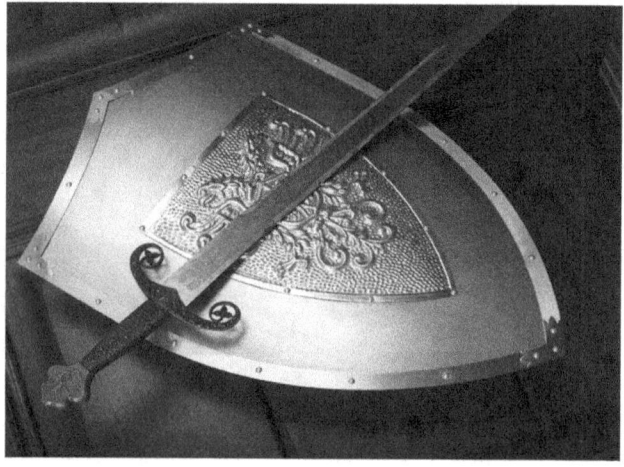

A Biblical Insight About God's Justice
and the Protocol of God as the Great King and Judge

WYNETTE A. TYRRELL

www.ingramcontent.com/pod-product-compliance
Lightning Source LLC
Chambersburg PA
CBHW062038120526
44592CB00035B/1264